TAROT

FOR BEGINNERS

A Practical Guide to Learning Psychic
Tarot Card Reading and Understanding
the Meanings

By
Abigail Welsh & Edson Keenan

TAROT FOR BEGINNERS

© Copyright 2020 - All rights reserved.

The content contained within this book may not be reproduced, duplicated or transmitted without direct written permission from the author or the publisher.

Under no circumstances will any blame or legal responsibility be held against the publisher, or author, for any damages, reparation, or monetary loss due to the information contained within this book. Either directly or indirectly.

Legal Notice:

This book is copyright protected. This book is only for personal use. You cannot amend, distribute, sell, use, quote or paraphrase any part, or the content within this book, without the consent of the author or publisher.

Disclaimer Notice:

Please note the information contained within this document is for educational and entertainment purposes only. All effort has been executed to present accurate, up to date, and reliable, complete information. No warranties of any kind are declared or implied. Readers acknowledge that the author is not engaging in the rendering of legal, financial, medical or professional advice. The content within this book has been derived from various sources. Please consult a licensed professional before attempting any techniques outlined in this book.

By reading this document, the reader agrees that under no circumstances is the author responsible for any losses, direct or indirect, which are incurred as a result of the use of information contained within this document, including, but not limited to, — errors, omissions, or inaccuracies.

TAROT FOR BEGINNERS

Table of Contents

Introduction v

Chapter One - History Of Tarot Cards 1

Chapter Two - How To Get Started 25

Chapter Three - Types Of Tarot Cards 44

Chapter Four - Meaning Of Tarot Cards 59

Chapter Five - Common Tarot Spreads 134

Chapter Six - Glossary.. 150

Final Words... 159

INTRODUCTION

Tarot cards are a fascinating tool that people use in a multitude of ways, ranging from seeking spiritual guidance and inner wisdom all the way to simple fun and enjoyment. Unfortunately, this range of use has led to a lot of confusion around tarot. Some people consider tarot cards to be "New Age garbage" that has caught on for the same reasons as astrology and palm reading. In complete contrast are those who claim that tarot card reading involves occult powers and should never be taken lightly. Among this latter group include those who might have studied tarot card history and their use in various religious practices, but also those who don't really understand what the "powers" they are talking about even mean.

There is a path between these two approaches. That is one that respects these beliefs, whether or not they are personally believed. This middle path allows for an objective look at both sides of this belief and can look at the history, purpose, and use of tarot cards without either belittling or over-exaggerating their function. We will be following this path throughout this book. I will try to help believers and non-believers understand how tarot cards are used and why. It is my hope that this will help more people grasp this practice with sensitivity, rather than being confused by half-truths and misunderstandings.

Regardless of whether or not you believe in the occult aspect to them, tarot cards are intriguing and beautiful. Tarot card decks are primarily composed of the same cards the same way that a deck of playing cards is. But, just as you can buy many different looking playing cards, there are thousands of different designs for tarot cards that you can choose from. We'll be covering how to pick your deck in chapter two for more on this topic. Beyond the fact that they are interesting to look at, there is something very cool about watching someone use a tarot card deck properly. While there may be an occult occurrence happening in such a moment, there can be no doubt that a large aspect of any kind of reading is a psychological one in which the true desires of the self come out. This fascinating area is one of the reasons for tarot card use that we'll be exploring more in chapter one.

One of the problems with getting into tarot cards these days is the fact that there is a lot of information to learn, but also an equal number of people who seem to be spreading misinformation. If you play a game of cards or a board game with people you know, you may well have your own rules, and these are called house rules. They are representative of one group's approach to the game, but not to the game as a whole. While not a game, this seems to have happened with tarot cards to a large degree. While there is nothing wrong with following the ways your cards pull you, it isn't the same as saying, "This is how it is supposed to be done." So, acquiring a lot of good information in a sea of misinformation can be a challenge to overcome.

In this book, we'll cut through the mistruths and boil a lot of information down into an easy to understand package. In order to do this, the book will follow a simple structure that builds on the information given in a natural fashion. We'll start with the history, myths, and purpose of tarot cards in chapter one. Chapter two will teach you how to get started with advice for picking your deck and questions to ask, as well as choosing which spreads to use and exploring how the position of a card affects its meaning. From there, chapter three will look at the different types of decks and the meaning of 'major arcana" and "minor arcana." Together, chapters two and three will give you what you need to choose and use a deck. Chapter four moves into understanding the cards and the meaning of both the major and minor arcana cards. With the cards in hand, we'll use chapter five to not only learn about some of the common spreads, but we'll walk through them with easily understandable directions so you can begin using your brand new deck.

With all this information to cover, there will likely be a few words that will confuse you. You might be scratching your head already at terms like "spread" or "major arcana." While one approach to writing is to stop and explain each new term as soon as it is encountered, this would hinder the flow of the book. In order to make it easy to follow along, a glossary has been included as chapter six. While we'll be covering most of the terms naturally in each of the sections directly related to them, this glossary will provide you with a way to brush up on terms and get a jump-start on your tarot knowledge.

So, if you're ready to cut through all the confusion and get right to the heart of the cards, flip to the next page and dive into the history of tarot cards.

CHAPTER ONE

HISTORY OF TAROT CARDS

One of the most fascinating things about tarot cards is how long they have been around. They're often described as "New Age nonsense," but there is nothing new about them. In fact, tarot cards can trace their history back roughly six hundred years. That makes them centuries older than anyone who ever called them New Age!

In this chapter, we'll explore their history to see where tarot card reading came from. This will be a great way to see how the practice has developed and changed over its long history. Speaking of changing, we'll also be looking at a ton of myths about tarot cards so we can change any mistaken preconceptions we've had about them. Finally, we'll look at the meaning and purpose that people find from using tarot cards. With all this in place, you'll have a much easier time deciding if tarot cards are for you or not. If they are, then stick around because we'll start learning to pick and use them in chapter two.

The Origin of Tarot Cards

In contrast to the New Age misunderstanding, there is a similar belief that circles around them. These cards are often described as being ancient. This is simply not true. They have quite a fascinating history, but they only go back a few hundred years. This may be considered ancient to some people living today, but in technical terms, we would need to go back a couple of thousand years to reach an ancient age. There is another misunderstanding which is attached to this one. It is often reported that the use of tarot cards can be traced all the way back through this history. To a degree, this is correct; the cards were used after all. However, the way they are used has continued to alter throughout history, and so our modern version of tarot card use is nothing like their original purpose.

While the most common use of tarot cards today is divination, aka reading the future, this wasn't always the case. There is a long history of tarot cards being used for divination, but they did not start this way, and the process of performing divination through tarot has evolved and grown as well. This is reflected in the evolution of the tarot deck throughout history. If you start to look into the past of tarot cards, you will find all sorts of decks with artwork that contrasts with the expected style of tarot cards. It was only in the last two hundred years or so that the tarot card deck started to take on its modern form. Prior to this, the symbols used by the cards were often changing. There were two major factors affecting this shift. The first was time. As time caused changes in society and the world, the deck altered and evolved naturally and would often have cards that reflected issues of the time. The other element contributing to this evolution was that tarot cards became international. They started in Italy, but it wasn't long before they were all over the globe.

It is suspected that tarot cards began as cards for a Mamluk game out of Turkey. At that stage, they weren't yet in a form we would recognize. While this game was being brought into Europe, it would be the Italian lords and counts which corrupted the Mamluk game and created the earliest version of the tarot in the years before 1500. Known as *tarocchi appropriati*, this was actually a card game rather than a method of divination. Players were dealt cards at random. Each card had a figure on it, and a name, and these would be combined at random so that the player was never sure what figures they were going to get. Players would use the cards they were dealt in order to write poetry about each other. A card like the knight followed by death might end up as a tale about the tragic demise of a hero, while following it with the lovers may then suggest that love would spring out of death. The way these were laid out and displayed was referred to as *sortes*, which can be loosely translated as "destinies." This points towards their future use in divination and the use of spreads as arrangements for reading the cards.

While the poetic play of these cards had the roots of divination buried inside, the cards themselves were far from being considered mystical tools. Even while being used for *tarocchi appropriati*, these cards were primarily being used for another card game, which was more in line with those we play today like solitaire, poker, or bridge. Rich nobles had artists paint entire sets of these cards that represented kings and queens, swords and staves, coins, and wands. In time, these would see a few additions and become tarot cards as we know them today with 78 cards in a deck, which is then divided into a major and minor arcana. It is believed that these images had nothing to do with divination and everything to do with the way the game was played. Just like a royal flush is important to poker, cards like the king, death, and the fool were all important in the game that tarot cards were originally designed for. But not only that, these images were also being drawn from the world around the players. We might consider the fool and the king to be old-fashioned, but they were everyday experiences during the time of invention.

As time went on, the original purpose of the deck was essentially lost. We have records and can come up with a decent understanding of what might have been played, but for the most part, it is another chapter of history that is lost to us. Instead of the bridge-like card game, it was the *tarocchi appropriati*, which became the more widespread use. That makes sense when we consider the way these cards passed from nobility into the common population. The rules of the original game weren't spread around, but the rules of *tarocchi appropriati* were much more flexible. The order cards were played was entirely random, and it was up to the individual to divine their meaning. A shift started away from a rigidly defined system of use to one that was inspired by individuals. The lack of rules allowed for the injection of mythology and mysticism into the practice. For each person, their relationship to tarot cards might be mundane, but it might also be mystical. Every person has the ability to invest the deck with meaning and power. Although not intrinsic to the cards themselves, this nonetheless infuses them with a mystic quality, and it was this aspect that kept tarot cards being designed and created throughout for centuries after they had lost their original purpose.

The most commonly encountered tarot card deck was designed by William Rider, a publisher, and A.E. Waite, a mystic, in 1909. While this deck has been in circulation since then, never coming out of print, this was made possible by the First World War and the rise in spiritualism that came with it. As mothers and fathers were losing their sons to the war, mysticism became a subject for popular exploration by famous writers like Arthur Conan Doyle, as well as scientists like Sir Oliver Lodge and Sir William F. Barrett. The Rider-Waite deck had especially prescient timing as it came out just before the war, and it came packaged with a book that taught how the cards were to be used in divination. Waite's belief in mysticism and divination fuelled a lot of the book, but Rider's smooth thinking created a sense of unity within each suit of the deck, so there was a sense of narrative flow in the cards themselves before an individual brought their own interpretation. That made it easier for people to follow the process of divination and understand what was being drawn. But, while this created the tarot deck as we think of it, it didn't reach the levels of popularity it has today until the late 1970s.

The rights of the Rider-Waite deck eventually passed into the hands of Stuart Kaplan, a businessman who sold copper mines for a living. Not just the copper itself, but the entire mine. He was in Germany at the same time that a toy fair was going on, and so he stopped to find something for his children. It was there he first encountered tarot cards. In his language, he describes these cards as having an almost supernatural effect on him. He was compelled by them. Not only did he gain the publishing rights to release the deck, but he began to study their history and, in 1977, released a book entitled *Tarot Cards for Fun and Fortune Telling*. His efforts clearly paid off because he was able to sell more than 200,000 tarot card decks, and he has gone on to release more books on the topic. Kaplan, as well as others, has run into a bit of an issue when it comes to exploring the history of these cards. Those that use them for divination claim tarot began with mystical origins, but the historical evidence doesn't support this reading. It has led to a bit of a confusing sphere around the topic, as some see this as an insult to their belief rather than simply being the truth. Nonetheless, while the mystical aspects of the tarot deck really found their home with the Rider Waite deck and Stuart Kaplan's advocacy of them since the late '70s, there have been a few signs which point to a deeper occult history than this story has previously revealed.

Waite was a famous mystic at the time that he worked with Rider to make the 1909 edition of tarot cards. While it would be perfectly fine to make the assumption that Waite simply took something he had seen before and added mystic qualities to it through promotion, this would be a simplification of this design process. It also overlooks an important part of A.E. Waite's life. Waite wasn't a charlatan in the way that P. T. Barnum or the Psychic Readers Network's Miss Cleo was. Waite is remembered today for two key reasons. The first is that he helped to invent the Rider-Waite tarot deck. The second is that Waite was one of the first modern historians to attempt a methodical study of Western occultism. Waite wasn't just somebody that was making things up as he went along. He was studying the origins of Western occultism as a spiritual tradition. Interested in the history of spiritualism and similar beliefs, it is likely that Waite encountered some of the more mystical uses of the tarot deck in his travels. He certainly had researched enough to be able to base the Rider-Waite deck after one of the oldest surviving tarot decks in existence. If this is the case, then Waite likely knew about some of the following mystical beliefs around the tarot deck.

Invented in the 1400s for use in a card game, by the 1700s, tarot cards were popping up more often for mystical purposes. While they had started in Italy, they had spread out over Europe by this point. Along with the spread of the cards came a spread of misinformation. Antoine Gébelin wrote about them in France, stating they were discovered in ancient Egyptian religious texts and had been brought into Europe by the wandering Romani peoples. Possibly compelling at the time, the interesting part of this argument isn't how it relates to the history of the tarot card, but what it says about interest in Egyptology at that time. Egypt was becoming a fascinating area of research and popular discussion. To many, Egypt was a place of mysticism, curses, and monsters. It was easy to believe that this strange deck of cards came from such a land. However, this would be impossible considering the fact that tarot cards had been in Europe long before the Romani people were. Not only that, but the Romani people came from Asia, and didn't have anything to do with Egypt or Africa. Regardless of this fact, this origin story was widely spread for years, and it may be responsible for a large portion of the change that tarot cards underwent at the time.

The first book on the subject would come out in 1791. Translated as Etteilla, or the Art of Reading Cards, author Jean-Baptiste Alliette discussed how he learned to divinate through a deck of 32 tarot cards and could read the future. In our world, the tarot deck is the most commonly used way to read the future through cards, but there were several other methods used throughout history. Alliette would go on to reinforce the Egyptian connection, while also making many points to differentiate it from the Egyptians to infuse his own mystic beliefs into the deck. Alliette's book would lead to a rise in interest in the supernatural qualities that had spawned dozens of books during his lifetime and thousands since.

While this history might seem to suggest there isn't any mystic quality to tarot card reading, I think that this would be an immature reading. Rather, one of the elements that sticks out in this history is the way that these cards have grown and changed organically as they have passed through history from hand to hand. What started as a simple game has managed to grow into a mystical practice. Does the fact that it was a game deduct anything from this evolution? I don't think so. Instead, I believe that we should be paying more attention to the fact that there are hundreds of different ways that objects have been used to read the future. From grains of sand to a thousand different card-based decks that have evolved over time, humanity has always used systems of controlled randomness to predict the future. I don't think it is so much the cards themselves that hold power, but, rather, it is the way in which individuals invest their own beliefs and mystic understandings into the cards. In a way, the power has been inside of us this whole time, and the tarot cards merely offer us one method through which we can tap into our inner forces.

Myths About Tarot Cards

TAROT FOR BEGINNERS

Just as the history of the tarot card seems to be misunderstood in the popular consciousness, it is safe to say that tarot cards themselves are the subject of confusion and misunderstanding. Growing up, I heard a lot of conflicting information about tarot cards, and they prevented me from exploring the topic for several years. It wasn't even that the information I was seeking was that difficult. I only wanted to know which deck I should purchase if I were going to get one. After all, there's a massive variety of decks on the market these days. This was a simple question, but the answers I got back made it more complicated than it should be. We'll tackle these myths that I encountered first hand, as well as many that are widely shared across the internet. We'll peel back each of these myths like layers of an onion. Once we get through all of the pieces that are mistakenly shared, we will then close out the chapter by looking at the real reasons people still use tarot cards in the year 2020.

Tarot Cards Are Evil and Occult: While tarot cards date back much further, if we remember that they became most popular from 1977 onwards, then we can easily deduce where this myth came from. The "Satanic Panic" of the 1980s saw accusations that schools, churches, governments, and other institutions were dens of Satanism. Supposedly true accounts of Satanic activity led to many things being called evil. Heavy metal music, video games, early *Dungeons & Dragons*, and tarot cards were just some of the things that were posited as allowing Satanic influence over children and young people. Tarot cards are seldom considered evil nowadays, but they still get grouped with the occult. While tarot cards can be used for occult purposes, so can anything. But, in their intended use, tarot cards are simply cards. Any power they have comes from the person that is using them.

Tarot Cards are Magical: Following on from that last sentence, a simple consideration of their production should reduce any traces of the magical. You can find many different tarot card decks in bookstores. These need to be shipped, packaged, and printed en masse. This particular myth is most likely due to films and television shows which present tarot cards as having power within themselves. This same myth had my mother break my ouija board when she found it. She said she didn't want dark magic in the house. But, she allowed Monopoly by Milton Bradley, the same company that made the ouija board. Unless you have a deck that was personally made by the artist, tarot cards are mostly mass-produced. Again, it's you who brings the power. Not the cards.

You Must Buy Your Own: This is one that tripped me up when I was younger. I was looking at some tarot cards in the bookstore. A friend offered to get me some for my birthday. But I had heard someone mention you have to buy your own, so I turned my friend down and never ended up with a set from that store. There are a lot of people that spread this rumor, but it does make a lot of sense. When you buy your own cards, you browse the selection and find the set that calls to you. If you are going to invest these cards with meaning and intent, then this will make it even more powerful because there is already something there between you and the cards. While this can be a powerful connection, it doesn't make gifted tarot cards any less powerful. In fact, it might come as a surprise, but this connection is seen in many of our purchases. When we browse a bookstore in general and walk away with something we found, there is a deeper connection to that item than when we are gifted a book. We can read them both the same, but the connection to the book we bought is all ours, while the connection to the gift is a link to the gift-giver. This is a subconscious emotional investment we often make. It can help us to feel connected to our cards, but it is in no way a requirement for using tarot cards.

Tarot Cards Must Be a Gift: This is the reverse of the previous myth. In this twist, it is the connection to the gift-giver that people see as being powerful. Which connection you think is more potent or significant is up to you, but that is all this is.

You're a Psychic if You Can Read Tarot: If you are a psychic, then you are going to have a much stronger relationship to your tarot deck, and you will likely use it in a much different way than most people. But if this were true, then we would have a world with too many psychics for anyone to have missed the memo! Tarot reading isn't so much about psychic powers as it is about intuition, random chance, and perception. In a lot of ways, it is a way of asking the universe a question and receiving an answer. It might not be the answer you want, or you might not even understand it properly. But each of us has a connection to the universe since we all exist within it. This is not a psychic activity but an intimate one.

Others Shouldn't Touch Your Cards: This is one of those myths that sound more like something out of a television series than reality. The idea here is that if somebody else touches your cards, then that will drain them of your power or any power you were able to work through them. But this is not true; the power resides within you and not the cards. Of course, you probably don't want to be handing them over to your friend if he's got Dorito dust all over his fingertips, but that applies to any object we value, and has nothing to do with the power in the cards. After all, somebody had to package them and get them from the factory to the store shelf.

Cats Suck the Power Out of Cards: This is a particularly odd myth. It goes against the Western connection of cats with the occult and instead plays off the ancient Egyptians' relationships with cats. They loved their cats and had complex relationships with them, but one of the pieces of Egyptian lore that passed into the popular consciousness is that cats had the ability to send the souls of the dead to the underworld. To some degree, this got incorporated in the mythology around tarot cards, very likely due to the misguided Egyptian connection we touched upon in the history section. It should be noted that while ancient Egyptians worshipped Bastet, a cat goddess, and put people to death for harming cats, this relationship to the dead is entirely constructed by British Egyptologists. Film scholar Douglas E. Cowan discusses this at length by looking at Egyptian mummy movies and shows how this particular myth was invented.

You Need to Wrap Your Cards in…: Some people finish the sentence with silk, others finish it with wool. Some say it needs to be leather, while others say that leather or anything that came from an animal will ruin the magic of the cards. But these cards don't have magic that needs to be brought to them by an individual. If you think they look best in leather, then wrap them in leather. Or silk or wool or anything else that either gives them a deeper meaning to you or that makes them look nicer in your opinion. Nobody else can tell you what to do with your cards, because they have a different perspective and relationship to their deck than you do with yours. Always follow your heart when dealing with tarot cards.

Tarot Cards Are Always Right: While many people that get a positive reading might wish this is true, those who get a negative reading can sigh in relief, knowing that it isn't. In a lot of ways, tarot cards are a way of asking questions of the universe. You may get back an answer, but it in no way means that the answer is correct. It might be that it is wrong from every angle, or it just might be wrong in the manner that you perceive it. More important than the answer the cards read is the answer the cards give you personally. We'll be talking about this more in just a moment. But the cards can be wrong, and they often are. This means that there is nothing in the cards that can cause you harm. A tragic reading in no way will cause you ill health or bad luck. You might experience bad luck and say that was what the reading was talking about, but this is your interpretation of the cards. They do not alter reality, but they change the way you think about your ongoing experience in a mindful manner.

The Death Card Means You Will Die: While many books and movies have insisted this to be true, it isn't the case. As dramatic as it is to pull out the death card, it doesn't mean death itself. In this sense, death is more of a metaphor. A person may get unlucky and experience a death in their family or friends after pulling a card, but this is pure chance. The card actually represents the end of something. We talk about the end of a relationship, the end of an era, the end of a work term. All of these could be described metaphorically as the death of a relationship, the death of an era, and the death of a job. These deaths are an end of one thing, but the beginning of another, and often, that new beginning is even more beautiful than imagined. So rather than worry about dying when you see the death card, you may be better off being excited about an upcoming change.

TAROT FOR BEGINNERS

So, Why Do People Use Tarot Card Readings Then?

This is both an easy and difficult question to answer. The easiest answer is to say that there are so many reason that it would be impossible to get into them all. But this is an unsatisfying answer because it doesn't really tell us anything about this practice. The reason there are so many different practices comes down to the individual nature of using tarot cards. There are guidelines on how to use them "properly," and we'll even be looking at a couple of these before the end of this book. But, since the power of tarot cards comes from the individual using them, there is no end to the list of reasons and ways that people use these cards.

Perhaps we can narrow this down to three key reasons. These are spiritual guidance, inner wisdom, and random fate. As we look at how each one of these functions, it is useful to keep in mind your reaction to each. You might find that you entirely lean towards one reason while considering another reason to be silly. These reactions are already telling you about the relationship you have with tarot cards, and they can help to point you towards the best way to use them personally. But you might also find that you are equally drawn and repelled by elements from each of these three reasons for using tarot cards. If these categories were each separate from one another, then this might cause some confusion, but it is best to consider these reasons as three circles on a Venn diagram. They can all overlap and interchange with each other, the borders between each only as thick or thin as the individual user perceives them to be.

Let's start with spiritual guidance. In this current age, we are faced with countless decisions every day. These can range from what you should wear to where you should shop, how you should think, how you should act, what you should eat, what you should read or watch, and countless others. Unfortunately for us, humans are quite poor at dealing with too many choices, and so our current world has a habit of making us feel very overwhelmed, anxious, or spiritually lost. We'll talk about using tarot cards to live true to our nature in a moment, but spiritual guidance is necessary in those dark times where we lose sight of our nature. When we are unsure of how to proceed, of what to do next, of how we can deal with everything around us, then tarot might offer a lot to us. Asking the universe for advice and guidance can help us to find our way back onto the path we were supposed to be living. When used in this manner, the tarot deck is treated with a spiritual power, as if it was a direct link to the greater universe itself. Individuals can invest limitless power and meaning into this connection, and it can be a positive force in overcoming hardship and staying in touch with their spiritual selves.

TAROT FOR BEGINNERS

Those that use tarot cards to access their inner wisdom share a lot of DNA with those that are after spiritual guidance. Inner wisdom already exists inside of us; that's why it's inner. But just because it is in there doesn't mean that we always have such an easy time accessing it. Have you become angry and realized that you were over-reacting yet still couldn't stop what you were doing? This is a common experience for most of us, especially when we are younger, which perfectly shows the way we can become disconnected from our inner wisdom. In the case of being angry, we could see the wisdom, but we couldn't act on it. A lot of times, we aren't even able to see our own wisdom. Sadness, work deadlines, groceries to buy, so many different obligations and emotional experiences, block our ability to perceive this wisdom. Using the tarot deck is one way we can get back in touch with this wisdom. As you do your reading, you pay attention less to what the cards are saying and more to the way you are reacting to what they say. If you can, try to notice that what they say is being made up inside of you as they are revealed. When we aren't sure of what we want, sometimes we do something like roll a dice or flip a coin to decide our path, and it is only once we see the result that we realize which direction we truly wanted to be pulled. Tarot cards are a more complicated version of this experience that can be used to tackle larger issues. In this method, the tarot cards are being used to help clear a way through everything that is blocking you from the wisdom that was in you all along.

TAROT FOR BEGINNERS

Many of those that view the tarot deck as random fate still find plenty of joy in using it. Like a dice roll or a flipped coin, a tarot deck might simply be consulted to see what happens in a matter that isn't overly important. This view may also see tarot cards as a game, a fun distraction in line with pulling a rabbit out of a hat or getting their palm read at the local fair. Many tarot card readers consider this approach to be disrespectful, but one person's lack of belief should not invalidate another's. Tarot cards themselves are not magic in any way. The power that they hold is deeply personal, and so if someone does not feel that power, then that only speaks about their relationship to tarot cards and not tarot cards themselves. As an interesting addendum, the randomness that comes from looking at the deck without meaning finds some uses in those that are interested in Chaos magic. Randomness and uncertainty is a major theme of those beliefs, and randomly pulling from a tarot deck can take on a lot of meaning because there is no further meaning beyond the rule of chance. That said, many in this community find that 78 cards are too restrictive to represent true chaos.

Regardless of which camp you find yourself in, neither is better or worse than another. What is important is that you approach tarot cards from your own unique, personal perspective, and you use this to guide your relationship to the cards. If you're excited to get your hands on some cards, then you're going to want to jump into chapter two right away.

Chapter Summary

- Tarot cards are often thought to be a New Age invention, but they actually date back several hundred years. They began in the form of a card game that slowly morphed into a fortune-telling game.

- Tarot cards took on their modern form in the early 1900s and have continued in this manner since.

- The most common tarot deck is the Rider-Waite deck that set the mold for the modern deck.

- There are many myths surrounding tarot cards, which can make it hard for people to get started.

- Tarot cards are not evil and, while some people use them for occult purposes, they are not themselves occult objects.

- Tarot cards aren't magical, either. A person may bring their own magic to it, but this comes from the person and not the cards.

- There is a myth that you must buy your own tarot cards, but this isn't so.

TAROT FOR BEGINNERS

- There is another myth that you have to be gifted a set of cards, and this is also false.

- Some people think that only psychics can read the tarot, but this doesn't make any sense.

- It is fine to let people touch your cards; that won't take away your power.

- Cats don't drain tarot cards of their power. The power comes from you.

- You can store your tarot cards however you like.

- Tarot cards aren't always right, and they can be easily misunderstood, too.

- Drawing the death card does not mean that you or anybody else is about to die.

- There is no right or wrong way to use the tarot deck so long as what you do feels right. However, there are some general reasons that people consult their decks: spiritual guidance, inner wisdom, and random fate.

- Some believe that the cards are a way to access higher spiritual guidance, and they use them as a way to infuse this into their lives.

- Others use the cards to discover wisdom and desires that were inside of them all along, using the cards as a way to read their true selves.

- Others use the cards as a way to speak to the universe, to invite the randomness of the cards to help guide them through life.

In the next chapter, you will learn how to pick your very first tarot card deck. If you have a deck, then you're going to want to ask it questions, so we look at how to choose questions that are right for tarot. We'll look at picking a spread and what the position of the cards mean when they are laid out. You'll have everything you need to start laying cards, but not the knowledge necessary to interpret the results. You'll need to read chapter four and the meanings of cards for that information.

CHAPTER TWO

HOW TO GET STARTED

If you're still reading, then that means tarot interests you enough to want to learn how to do it yourself. That's wonderful. With something as personal as tarot card reading, the only way to truly understand it, and get a sense for how it fits into your life, is to try it yourself. We've already talked about the many reasons why all the misinformation about tarot cards makes it hard to get started, so we can skip all of that. In this chapter, we will get straight to the point so that you can pick your first deck and start preparing yourself for your very first reading.

Don't worry; it's going to be a lot easier than people make it sound.

How to Pick Your First Deck of Tarot Cards

TAROT FOR BEGINNERS

When it comes to picking your first deck, there doesn't need to be any mysticism or magic surrounding it. If somebody has given you a deck of tarot cards as a gift, then you are going to be perfectly fine using those. That is, you will be fine using them if they are comfortable for you. Picking out a deck of tarot cards is pretty much the same as picking out anything - you want to find something that will match you. If you have big feet, then you purchase big shoes, after all! We'll look at these practical considerations, but first, let's return to the idea of connection.

As you browse for your first deck, you are going to see all sorts of different shapes and sizes, colors, and designs. You may be keeping in mind physical considerations such as the size of the cards themselves, but you should keep yourself open as you browse. A central part of picking your deck of tarot cards is to follow the energy that forms through the connections you make to the deck. If you see a deck that calls to you, that is the deck you should go with. If it is bigger or smaller than you first intended to purchase, that isn't going to matter. The fact that it called to you will make all of these considerations seem pointless. When it comes to tarot cards or other ways in which we tap into spiritual guidance or inner wisdom, it is important to follow the energy of connection whenever it shows itself.

TAROT FOR BEGINNERS

Beyond connection, probably the biggest consideration you are going to make is the artwork and imagery on the cards. Some tarot card decks go with a minimalist design, others may inject elements of science fiction. Many are done in medieval artwork styles, which give the cards a feeling of folk roots and historical connection. The artwork on your cards doesn't affect the way that you use them. It is entirely up to you what your cards look like, but you should consider how a new design or something as extreme as a science fiction inspired design will affect the way you personally feel when using your cards. Remember, too, that if you do readings for other people, a newer style may throw them off. A lot of people think that tarot cards are ancient mystical tools and so it may lead to better readings by sticking with an old-fashion design rather than a new one. It's always helpful to consider both sides of the experience.

As already mentioned, tarot cards come in different sizes. Some can be as large as a hardcover book, while others are the size of playing cards. How large your cards are will impact upon how much space is required to use them. It will also make it harder or easier to shuffle them depending on the size of your hands. If you want to make your deck stand out from a pack of playing cards, then it can be fun to get cards that are just a slight bit larger. They'll still be quite easy to shuffle, but they will feel a little bit different when held, and this will allow you to associate this new card size with your tarot cards.

This is an easy trick to make your tarot cards stand out and form a deeper bond inside your subconscious.

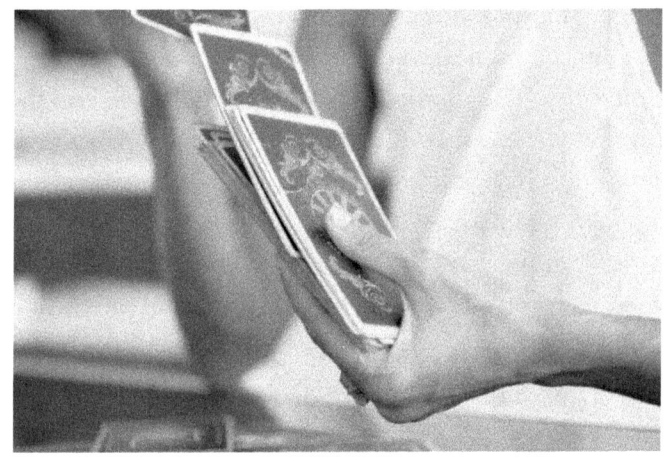

Finally, you should also consider the quality of the cards. If they are $2.99, there's probably a reason. Cheap cards will work just as well as high-quality cards do when it comes to readings, but they are going to rip, tear, crease, and stain far easier. You will likely also find that cheaper cards just don't seem to shuffle properly for some reason. Rather than each card being an entity unto itself, cheap cards like to get stuck together, and then tear when you try to separate them. This is OK if you're just purchasing some playing cards, but tarot cards require a connection, and it is hard to form a close link with a deck of cards that is constantly falling apart on you. It may cost a lot more to get a high-quality deck, but it will last much longer and cause far less frustration.

But even with all that said, remember that your connection to your deck is uniquely yours. If your first deck of tarot cards were cheap and always breaking, then maybe that is how you think of your cards, and so you only purchase cheaper decks. All those reasons that are frustrations for one person could be pluses to another. When it comes to you and your cards, follow the feeling in your gut. That feeling is more significant than any of the other concerns we've covered.

Asking Questions: What to Ask and How to Do It

The purpose of tarot cards is to reach spiritual or inner wisdom, and the only way that we can do that is through asking questions. If we didn't bring a question to the tarot reading, then we can't expect to find any answers. Asking the right question is so vital to having a successful and productive tarot reading. If you ask the wrong questions, then you are going to find yourself confused with answers that don't make sense or upset with answers that don't reflect your true intentions and desires. There aren't any rules as to whether one question is right and one question is wrong. Since what is in your heart is more important than any single rule could be, there would be no point. But there are some easy to follow steps that we can take to make sure we are asking questions that open us up to the full spectrum of the tarot instead of limiting ourselves to a disappointing experience.

What you want to learn from the tarot deck will be determined by you. There is no limit to what you can ask from it. You might meet somebody that uses theirs exclusively in matters relating to their career, another person with matters only of the heart. Your relationship to the tarot deck will be uniquely yours. So the content of the questions will almost entirely be up to you with no limitations whatsoever. Instead, the issue doesn't come from what we want to ask the tarot deck, but the way we go about doing it. We want to ask questions in a manner that is fitting of the tarot deck and the way that it performs. This means we'll want to avoid closed questions, stay within our own consciousness, focus on the now, and be proactive, and accountable to ourselves and the deck. These aspects may sound complicated, but they're easy to do, and once you start asking questions in this manner, you'll find that the deck is much more approachable and inviting.

When it comes to asking the universe questions, tarot cards have a lot of flexibility in their ability to answer. To make a comparison with a retro favorite, a magic eight ball has a total of 20 answers for the questions you ask of it. The tarot deck provides between 76,000 and 456,000, depending on how you consider the minor arcana cards. You can ask a magic eight ball a yes or no question, and you have a pretty good chance of getting back a yes or no answer. But with the tarot deck, you are going to get back much longer and much more complicated responses. With such a large range of possible answers, it is essential that we consider how open our questions are.

Closed questions have only a small number of possible responses. "Will you marry me?" is a closed question because the only answers are "yes," "no," and "I need time to think about it." "What time is it?" is a closed question because the only appropriate answer is the time or a close approximation of it. Most of the questions that we ask are closed questions, with a specific goal in mind. In contrast, open questions allow for much deeper answers. If you asked, "Will my book get purchased?" then you will get back a yes or no. If you ask the much more open version of the question, "What can I do to make sure that my book sells?" then you have opened up the range of answers. It could be to hire a marketing firm or take a class on digital promotion. You may need to research your niche in more depth to bring a perspective that is lacking from the competition. It may be to follow up on emails with that publisher you had been speaking to. The end goal of the question is the same, you want a book that sells, but the way you reach it is open. This is great for our psychology and perspectives because it makes us much more fluid and adaptable when plans change. Plus, it is great for the tarot because it allows it to answer with its full depth and flexibility. It may seem weird to ask questions this way, but once you get used to it, you'll see improvements in your readings and often even your life.

Sticking with your own consciousness is important when practicing tarot cards, regardless of your relationship to the deck. If you channel your own energies and magic through the deck in your readings, then it is inappropriate to do readings about other people without their consent. However, if you are using the tarot to tap into inner wisdom, then you might be able to understand why this won't work for you either. Any inner wisdom the deck allows you to reach has to come from inside you to begin with. You are your own person, a single consciousness. You do not have the ability to access another person's consciousness in order to speak for them and see their lived truth. This means you will never be able to properly ask a question about another and get a real answer. The answer you receive will always be in error because it will be your interpretation of a person's wants and desires rather than any truth from the universe or the cards. Even when you do a reading for another person, it will largely be the individual that interprets and makes sense of the reading you perform for them.

So, if you want to stay with your own consciousness, then your questions should reflect this. You might want to know about the way your boss is feeling, or if the apple of your eye has their heart set elsewhere. Regardless, think not about them, but about how you relate to the situation. If you're asking about your boss because you're after a promotion, then cut to the source and ask what you can do to impress your boss. This is focused on the self, whereas, "Does my boss respect me?" is focused on the other person. Staying with yourself will allow you to keep the focus where it truly matters. You aren't asking the tarot deck questions for other people; you are asking because they have an impact on you. Make sure that you always ask from within your own conscious experience, so that you can get straight to the core of why the question is important in the first place.

Just as we must stay with ourselves, it is necessary we remain in the present as well. While we often use the tarot cards to look towards what we should do, we don't use the deck to predict the future or focus on the past. Everything that has happened has already come to pass, so the tarot can tell you nothing about them that you don't already know. Everything that is to come can be changed at a moment's notice by world events, personal events, or worse. We exist in the now, and this is where we are most able to access the wisdom of the tarot. Since we live in the now, it is our actions in the present that build the future we come to inhabit. We often forget about the present because we get so lost in the past or the future, but if we remember that the tarot deck is most powerful when approached through the present, then not only will we ask better questions, but we will find a lot more time on our hands than we knew we had. When we start living in the present, our world begins to look a lot bigger and filled with many more opportunities.

Focusing on the present is not hard. Rather than asking questions such as, "What will happen next?" or, "Was that the best action I could have taken?" you should ask questions such as, "What can I do to make sure events work in my favor?" or, "How can I treat this outcome in a positive manner?" When you start to focus your questions on the present around you, you will find that you begin to get answers which you can put into action, and that you stop trying to imagine the future, and instead, you start to build it. As you are getting ready to ask a question, stop, and consider if it is one in which you are focused on yourself in the present. When you are stopping and doing this, you will naturally be more accountable to yourself and to the deck.

Being accountable to the deck and yourself means you ask questions that are within your control and capability. If you have never once picked up a paintbrush, then a question such as, "Am I going to be a famous painter?" is going to be breaking this guideline (as well as being a closed question about the future). If you asked, "What can I do to improve my painting skills?" then you are going to have a much better result. Rather than fabricate a version of reality in which you achieve something outside of your control, you instead search for the answers that are going to provide you with the necessary advice and actions needed to live more fully. The tarot deck does not change the future, and so if you aren't being honest and accountable in your questions, then you will find that you never have an easy relationship with your deck. Dishonesty and unrealistic expectations can leave you angry and frustrated with your deck and tarot cards in general.

When you follow these basic guidelines, you will find that the questions you ask the tarot cards are much more clear and direct. Since they're open rather than closed, you will be able to get complex answers and truly tap into the deep wisdom of the cards.

An Introduction to Tarot Spreads

People might talk about different spreads as if they had some inherent meaning in and of themselves. Part of this comes from the mystique of the name. If they were just called a layout, then it wouldn't sound nearly as cool, but, in reality, that it is all that a spread is. You could use a deck of tarot cards and lay them out in any order that is relevant to you, and you would technically be using them right. You might get on the nerves of people who are very particular in their own relationship to the cards, but you are free to create spreads in any way that is meaningful to yourself. When you are using a tarot deck, you are opening yourself up to an incredibly high amount of chance. If you are asking open-ended questions, then you will have a much easier time getting answers. This can be made even more likely through the use of a spread designed for the kind of question you are asking.

Since a spread is just a layout, there are spreads for love and careers. The cards are always the same, so what is being changed with a spread is not just the placement of the cards themselves, but the symbolic meaning they've been invested with. A very simple spread is to do three cards together for past, present, and future. A simple and fun trick for those learning tarot, it isn't a particularly valuable reading since we've already left the past behind, as discussed in the last section. By changing the meaning of each card by designating it a purpose in the reading, you have much greater control over the questions you can ask. If you have ever played one of those Mad Lib word games where you pick verbs and nouns to create funny stories, then this might seem familiar. Rather than filling out a single word, a card fills out the empty slot. Tarot cards are never easy to read, and so there are a lot of ways these readings can be interpreted, and it is far more complicated than those word games, but the principle behind it is the same.

We are going to be looking at how to do a few spreads of our own in chapter five, so we're not going to cover how each spread is done here. This would slow down our conversation and turn it into a series of steps to be followed. Using a spread is very easy, and you can find many of them for free across the internet with a little bit of Googling. What is more useful for our discussion right now is how to pick the right spread. You might have questions about work, and so a career spread probably sounds right up your alley. A love spread pretty much speaks for itself. But there are plenty of questions which these spreads don't work for. Sometimes, it isn't immediately obvious what kind of spread you should be using. Picking the right spread is going to be determined by what you want to ask, how much you want to know, and what you know already.

Starting with the question, you are going to want the spread you pick to be able to give you an answer. If I have a problem, then I might do a very straightforward three-card spread. The first card represents the nature of the problem, the second card is the cause of it, and the third card would be the solution. A simple three-card spread can be used for love, work, and pretty much anything else you want to ask. Seriously, a three-card spread is the easiest thing in the world, and you can always play with and adjust each piece. Adjusting them while asking the same question over a period of time can significantly help to open up your understanding of the cards and the question at hand.

Of course, since a three-card spread is so easy to adapt to everything, it can also feel very surface level. It never really seems to go deeply into a particular problem. It can be a great way to start investigating something with the tarot deck, but often you will find that you want to go a little bit further. It isn't even that you want to get more information, so much as you want it to be more specific to the task at hand. By distilling your problem into a question for the cards, you will understand the question enough to seek out an appropriate spread. If it's about love, life, health, wealth, fertility, spirituality, healing, or more, you will be able to find many spreads that fit. By understanding the question, you can pick the spread that will give you the most desirable information.

That information should be your next determining factor in which spread to use. We've talked about this in parallel in the previous paragraph. A spread that is more specific doesn't necessarily give you more detail, but most of them will. However, there are general purpose spreads that also allow for a lot of detail. The more detailed a spread is, the more the various cards are going to be interacting and influencing each other. That means that correctly reading a more complicated spread takes time. Time to learn, but also time to perform. We'll talk about time to learn in a moment, but time to perform is important to note because a complicated spread is always, by its very nature, going to take longer to read. This isn't a problem for many people, but it is good to remember because nothing is worse than a rushed reading, and even more so, one that is cut off right in the middle. The more detailed the answer you want, the longer and more complex the spread is going to be.

Finally, it is important to keep in mind how much you know and what you are comfortable with. If you are working with three-card spreads, then it is straightforward to read each part of the spread because they interact with each other in a sequential order. But more complicated spreads have complex interactions that can be modified, facilitated, or interrupted by other cards as they are revealed. The order in which each piece is revealed, and the position the card is in, as well as its place in the spread, all alter and change the meaning of the card. That can take a lot of time to read. If you are doing a reading for a friend, then it probably isn't a good idea to reach for a complicated spread that you haven't gotten much practice with yet. It is great to push yourself to try new things, but there is a time and a place where the old and reliable comes in handy.

The cool thing about tarot cards is that while it takes a while to learn what each card means and how they interact in a spread, once you do understand, it becomes a lot easier to read. With experience, you can make complicated spreads look easy. Start with some simple three-card spreads, or some of the spreads later on in chapter five. Once you feel comfortable reading a few different three-card spreads, start practicing with a more complicated variation, and working your way up. With practice and patience, you can read even the most difficult and complex ones like an expert.

Position of the Tarot Card

The position of the tarot card is going to change depending on the spread that you are using. More than anything else, this is going to have the biggest impact on the position of the card. If you are doing a three-card spread, then you will have three cards in a row, and their meanings change depending which is first, middle, or last. What that meaning is will come entirely from the spread itself.

Many spreads are done by placing the cards out in order, but some involve laying cards in odd positions either on purpose or by random chance. You may find that some cards invoke new meaning when they are reversed ("hiding") or turned on their side ("laying down"). We'll be looking at cards in detail in chapter four, and we'll see first-hand how each of the different cards has its meaning. How laying down or hiding affects each card is mostly in the eyes of the interpreter. There is no right or wrong to these, but they mostly help the reader to get a little deeper into the core of the answer.

Note that positions in a spread are very malleable. There are spreads that are taught in many different ways. A Celtic cross spread may assign vastly different meanings to the first four cards compared to what another reader believes them to mean. So if you start to read a spread in a manner that works for you, and someone tells you it's wrong, remember they are your cards and how you read them is between you and the cards. So long as you understand the position you are placing the card into, you are still on track. If you can understand how the spread works to provide an answer, then you are using your cards exactly as you are meant to.

Chapter Summary

- There are all sorts of different shapes and sizes and designs that you can choose from for your first deck of tarot cards.

- Look for a connection with your cards and choose based on this. This connection is the most important thing you can get from a deck.

- You may also want to pick a deck that has artwork that captures your attention.

- Tarot decks can come in large or small sizes, and so you should get a size that is comfortable for you and which you can use in the space available to you.

- Get high-quality cards rather than cheap cards so that you can have a longer-lasting and better experience and relationship with your deck.

- You can ask any question you want to the tarot deck, but if you ask your questions by following certain guidelines, they are more productive.

- Ask questions that are open and allow for many answers.

- Stick with questions about yourself and how you relate to others rather than asking questions about other people.

- Stay true to the fact that your actions are your own, and you have to be responsible for them.

- Stay in the present. You can look to the future, but don't forget where you are, and that action in the now is how you get to the then.

- Tarot spreads are ways of laying cards out so that they take on different meanings. Each space in a spread has a meaning that the card then comments on.

- Cards take on different meanings when they are in different places in a spread, or if they are laying down or upside down.

In the next chapter, you will learn about the many different tarot decks and how cards differ from each other. You will also learn about the major and minor arcana to see what these mean and how this affects the cards that fill them out.

CHAPTER THREE

TYPES OF TAROT CARDS

While a traditional tarot deck comes with 78 cards, this isn't always the case. Some people prefer to use a deck with only cards from the major arcana. This will create a more compelling and interesting reading, though not necessarily any more accurate than doing a reading normally. Regardless of whether you use both arcanas, or only one, there are many different types of tarot decks which you can choose from when picking your own. These range from the classic Rider-Waite deck through to the Angel Oracle deck or the Druid Craft deck. We'll be covering the differences between each of these in this chapter.

We'll also be looking at both the major and the minor arcana so that we can get a sense of what they are. With a name like "major arcana," your first assumption is likely to be based on the similarity to "arcane."

However, there isn't anything particularly supernatural about an arcana. Rather than deal with the occult, the arcanas are a way of dividing the tarot deck into two sections. We'll look at each of them carefully to close out this chapter. If you are looking for information on what each individual tarot card means, then you'll want to skip ahead to chapter four.

The Various Types of Tarot Card Decks

Since most tarot decks come with 78 cards, the choice of tarot deck should be made through your link to a particular deck. Being drawn towards the cards is crucial, as it lets you bond with your deck even before you get it open and have a chance to use it. But if you have been reading tarot cards for a while, then you've probably heard mention of a few different types of decks. A lot of people hear about them when they are first getting into tarot and are unsure of what to pick. Everyone suggests this or that kind of deck, and it quickly becomes overwhelming for a beginner. It is for this reason that we talked about choosing a deck based on how you connect to it first, rather than because it is of one particular kind or another.

Since you have your first deck now, we are safe to look into the different kinds. You may find one that draws you even more than your own deck does. If this is the case, then there is nothing wrong with you, your cards, or your desire. Many tarot users have multiple decks. Some they invest with an aura of love, only asking that deck questions of the heart. Another might be used for problems of the soul, another for issues in the career. Nothing says you need to settle for a single deck, so don't feel bad or overwhelmed if you find yourself wanting a second or even a third deck. The essential thing is you are enjoying yourself and finding meaning through your interactions with your decks. If that's the case, then you are doing great.

Each of the following decks includes 78 cards. That is 22 cards of the major arcana and 56 cards of the minor arcana, which are then divided up further into four suits that each has 14 cards. The biggest difference you will find between these decks is an aesthetic one. While the look of the cards doesn't have a direct impact on the reading in terms of which cards are drawn, they do impact the way that you interpret the cards. This impact is even greater in those you are reading for. The look and design of the cards are all a client has to go on if they don't know the meaning of the cards themselves. If you are using a bright and cheerful deck, then they are far more likely to take your reading lightly or in a positive direction. A darker, more twisted looking deck, is going to result in darker interpretations. Keep in mind that this is a subconscious effect that happens without either of you being aware of it directly. If you are only using one deck, then something neutral is a good way to go, not too cheerful, but not too dour either. This alone is a great reason to use multiple decks.

Speaking of multiple decks, there is nothing that says you need to use a single deck. You could combine cards from different decks or perform readings using two decks to answer the same question. While there are plenty of people who will see this as insulting, there are no laws against it. The only rule is what you feel in your heart and soul as you work with your cards. If you are drawn to use multiple decks together, then that's for you to follow. You might find that mixing two decks doesn't work, as different designs on the back of the cards can make it easy to tell which cards are which. However, you may take the major arcana from one deck and the minor arcana from another to create a whole new deck. You will be able to tell apart the major and minor arcanas, but not what each card is until it is drawn and revealed. A combination deck like this can easily work in many traditional spreads, though you will either need to search for or invent your spreads to use multiple decks together. Let the fact that creating new decks and new spreads is encouraged sink in. If someone is getting upset with you for how you use your tarot cards, then they're the one in the wrong because you are free to use the cards as you see fit. The connection is your own. Now, on to the decks.

We've already mentioned the Rider-Waite deck a few times throughout the book, so it makes sense to begin here. For many people, it is the cards from the Rider-Waite deck that they see in their heads when they hear somebody talk about tarot. As regards what has historically endured, the Rider-Waite deck is among the oldest of the tarot decks still in circulation. In fact, more Rider-Waite decks have been sold than any other single deck. Add the sales of the others together, and you still won't come close to the popularity of the Rider-Waite deck. Most of the decks seen in movies and television are Rider-Waite decks, and the artwork on the cards has become so famous that it graces the cover of many a rock album. The Rider-Waite deck is an excellent choice for a mostly neutral reading. Since the artwork of the deck has a medieval feeling, clients are more likely to accept Rider-Waite as a real occult tool rather than just a deck of cards. While not an occult tool, this does make the Rider-Waite a powerful device for performing readings for clients or friends.

Another famous deck is that of the Angel Oracle. The oracle deck is not actually a tarot deck in the traditional sense, so in many ways, it doesn't belong in this book. However, it is used to produce similar readings, and it is often lumped into discussions on the tarot, so we'll briefly consider it here. The Angel Oracle deck is the name for a specific kind of oracle deck. These decks are made of 36 cards that are split up into their own categories. These are form, creation, and paradise. Already, this stands in contrast with the 78 cards of the tarot, which are divided into the major arcana and the minor arcana, with the minor arcana further subdivided into four suits. Rather than the swords, cups, wands, or pentacles suits of the minor arcana, the oracle deck only uses its own three categories. With the Angel Oracle deck, the cards use images of divine angels for all the artwork. Each card also has an uplifting saying on it, so that it offers value even when you can't interpret the card itself. While these decks are often suggested as an easy way to get into tarot, they aren't actually tarot but are more like a spiritual sister. The Angel Oracle deck is particularly good for doing readings with Christians. While easier to learn, reading an oracle deck is a different skill from tarot card reading.

The Universal Marseille tarot deck is one of the more beautiful sets out there, in my humble opinion.

While Rider-Waite is more popular, the Universal Marseille deck traces its origins back much further. We saw that Arthur Waite had a lot of occult credibility when he was making the Rider-Waite deck (he was a member of the Hermetic Order of the Golden Dawn, after all), and so this led to that deck's old fashioned style. The artwork for that deck was created by Pamela Colman Smith. Smith, also known as Pixie, met Waite at a meeting of the Golden Dawn, and in 1909 they produced the deck with the help of Rider. While Waite and Pixie make for captivating biographies, they joined the party more than 150 years after the Universal Marseille deck did.

A man by the name of Claude Burdel invented this particular deck in 1751. He has been intrigued by a deck he encountered in Switzerland, and he was determined to make his own. Burdel didn't have immediate access to a printing press, so he looked around to see what he had to hand. This led to him making his deck entirely out of woodcuts. The influence of the artwork comes from the Swiss deck that he'd seen. The Universal Marseille deck is based on this woodcut deck that Burdel made in the 1700s. It has an even older style and aesthetic than the Rider-Waite deck, though there isn't the same mystical quality to the artwork. The artwork instead gives the impression of the Dark Ages, which is helped by the fact that it has very simple colors. Reds and blues are featured in abundance, with yellow for gold and trim. A little bit of green is included, but the cards are almost entirely kept in a three-color contrast. This gives them a brighter appearance than the Rider-Waite deck. That may allow for happier readers, though the deck is less likely to impress those that seek out tarot readings because they heard they were a supernatural practice.

A similar deck is the Renaissance Tarot Deck that Brian Williams designed. Williams' deck uses images inspired by the Greek gods. Each of the four minor arcana suits is represented by a particular mythological deity such as Cupid or Hercules. Where the Universal Marseille offers bright colors that stand out, the Renaissance Tarot Deck uses subdued colors that all blend into each other. You need to take a moment to really look at these cards to take in just how complicated the artwork is. This deck gives a precise tone, but the pastel colors do well for a reading in a comfortable setting, especially when asked about questions of love.

The Legacy of the Divine Tarot and the Druid Craft Tarot Deck both function under the same general idea. The Druid Craft Tarot Deck uses images inspired by Pagan ideas, so there are pregnant mothers and forest goddesses and lots of green tones. The Legacy of the Divine Tarot deck has a much more Postmodern appearance to the cards. These cards use loud colors that leap off the page, with imagery that evokes a modern-native feeling. Both of these decks are wildly popular, but their designs point towards the subculture that each is aimed at.

TAROT FOR BEGINNERS

One of the more interesting modern decks is The Wild Unknown Tarot. Kim Krans made this one, creating the art and writing the included guidebook. While the other modern tarot decks try to look either like they came from the past or use images that directly call to the past, the Wild Unknown Tarot is the only modern tarot deck that feels like it is done with the past and ready for what awaits in the present and the future. It conveys a sense of wild, unknown territory. However, this doesn't take away from the deck's power in the least. The cards focus more on the immediate family (husband, wife, father, mother, son, brother, sister, daughter), rather than on esoteric titles such as king or queen. Perhaps that creates a more grounded feeling to the cards. Speaking of which, the illustrations that Krans uses mix strong black and white roots with loud and vibrant colors that dance off each card. They are immediately eye-catching, without relying on the intricate detail that the Legacy of the Divine Tarot or the Druid Craft Tarot Deck does. You'll find beautiful nature scenes and a wide range of animals on the cards, but there are no humans in sight. This creates a timeless feeling to these modern cards and makes it clear why it is one of the best selling tarot decks ever made.

What is Major Arcana?

The tarot deck is divided into two sections with 22 major arcana cards and 56 minor arcana cards. This can be thought of as a division between the trump cards and the rest of the cards. Remembering that tarot cards get their root in card games, we can think of them a little bit like a regular deck of cards. In a deck of playing cards, there are four suits, and each of those suits has a joker, a queen, and a king. If we were to put this into terms of major or minor arcana, then the joker, queen, and king would be the major arcana while the 1, 2, 3, 4, 5, 6, 7, 8, 9, and 10 would all be the minor arcana. This is an easy way to think of the major and minor arcana, but there is one little problem with it. It isn't that smooth.

The problem with trying to make a one-for-one comparison with a pack of playing cards is the size of the decks. There are 78 cards in a tarot deck, but only 52 in a pack of playing cards, 54 if you count the two jokers. A pack of playing cards has 13 cards in each suit, but a tarot deck has 14 cards in each minor arcana suit. That gives us the 56 minor arcana cards, and we're already at a bigger sized deck compared to our playing cards. A further problem appears when we look at minor arcana and realize that these suits each have their jack, queen, and king. So, really, a pack of playing cards is a better way to understand the minor arcana cards rather than the deck as a whole. However, the trump card metaphor still stands.

A trump card is a card or a suit of cards that has been chosen to be more valuable than the other cards. In the game of blackjack, we treat ones, jacks, queens, and kings as trump cards when compared to the other cards. The 8 in a game of crazy eights is a trump card. In tarot cards, the major arcana is composed of trump cards that are more valuable than the minor arcana. This is likely due to tarot's origins from earlier card games. The cards in the major arcana are all named figures, each of which very likely had some role to play in the original function of the game, but that has since been lost. They came to be known as major or minor arcanas in the 1800s through the writing of Jean-Baptiste Pitois. Just exactly what is this occult significance to the major and minor arcanas seems to be fluid depending on where you look. Some claim it to come from Egypt, others from Italian origin.

For the most part, the major arcana are thought of as symbols that gain their meaning and value through metaphor and allegory. There are 22 major arcana cards, though they are labeled as 0-21 rather than 1-22. Figures in the major arcana range from The Fool to The Devil, The Lovers to The Chariot, and The Empress to The World. We'll be looking at all of these in more detail in the next chapter to see how they are interpreted and understood. But first, let's take a look at the cards in the minor arcana.

What is Minor Arcana?

Continuing from our previous section, we have already learned that the minor arcana is composed of 56 cards that are divided into four suits with 14 cards each. What each of these suits is called, and how it works in a particular deck, may differ from each other, but they work pretty much the same way regardless. The Latin sees these as wands, coins, cups, and swords, while the French see them as clubs, diamonds, hearts, and spades. Elemental based interpretations assign these as fire, earth, water, and air, while a class-based interpretation settled on artisans, merchants, clergy, and nobility.

Each of these suits is broken down into the same cards. Ace, two, three, four, five, six, seven, eight, nine, ten, page, knight, queen, and king. The page, knight, queen, and king are the trump cards of their particular suit, but these are all still trumped by any of the cards in the major arcana. More than anything else, the minor arcana cards are going to pop up most often to alter or impact the reading of a major arcana card. If the major arcanas are the big players, then the minor arcana are the staff and support that make it possible. Or, another way of thinking about it, the major arcana point to the big key elements and the minor arcana allows us to get a more accurate reading and understanding of the powers at play.

This is pretty much all there is to know about the minor arcana, though it is worth noting there are many camps of tarot reading which place a greater emphasis on the power of the minor arcana. The Order of the Golden Dawn, already deeply involved in the creation of the Rider-Waite deck, actually assigns each card number a celestial body to deepen their understanding of the deck through their own belief system. How much or how little power you assign to the minor arcana is up to you. To get a better understanding of what is right for you, we will need to explore the cards in depth. We turn our attention to this task in the next chapter.

Chapter Summary

- There are many different kinds of decks which you can use, many are the traditional 78 cards, but with different approaches or with the suits of face cards renamed.

- You can use more than one deck if you want, there is no reason why you can't.

- The most popular deck of all time is the Rider-Waite deck, which has a very traditional style to it.

- The Angel Oracle deck is extremely popular, but it isn't a tarot card deck; it is an oracle deck, which is an entirely different thing.

- The Universal Marseille tarot deck is based on old woodcuts.

- The Legacy of the Divine Tarot and Druid Craft Tarot Deck are two examples of modern-day decks that have a very New Age feeling to them.

- One of the more popular decks is The Wild Unknown Tarot, which uses rainbow colors and a focus on scenery that makes it feel both fresh and ageless.

- The major arcana is 22 cards that make up the fool's journey. These are face cards which each represent aspects of the self and of experience which we need to take into ourselves and learn from.

- The minor arcana is made up of 56 cards. These are then broken down into four different suits, each of which has 14 different cards.

In the next chapter, you will learn what each and every one of the 78 tarot cards that make up the major and minor arcana means so that, with a little bit of practice, you can read them like a pro.

CHAPTER FOUR

MEANING OF TAROT CARDS

At this point, you have learned the history of the tarot deck and seen the many different reasons that people use them. Having chosen your own, we've gone over what questions to ask, how to pick a spread, and how the meaning of a card changes depending on where it is located. All of this provides the basic training necessary to create the foundation of your new skill in reading tarot cards. But it is time for the hardest part.

There are 78 different cards in the tarot deck, and each of them has a meaning. These meanings take on whole new depth, depending on where they are placed in a spread. To fully understand and read a particular spread, you are going to need to understand what each of the cards does. Getting the cards down so that you know them by heart is difficult, but it is necessary that you do so prior to reading for others. Without knowledge of what they mean, you can't understand how they change and differ depending on their placement. To fully understand this, you need to understand both the spread you are working with and the cards that you have in your hand. We'll look at spreads in the next chapter; for now, we've got cards to explore.

This chapter is going to be jam-packed with information about all of these cards. There's 78 of them, after all. To make it a little easier to follow, we'll start by looking at the major arcana and then move onto the minor arcana. The cards in the minor arcana all alter and affect those in the major arcana, but it is the major arcana, which is the most complicated and important. Practice with your deck at home as you read along, quiz yourself on what each of them means by shuffling the major arcana cards and drawing them randomly. Take your best guess, then double-check the answer below. These will all be old friends in no time.

The Cards of the Major Arcana: At a Glance

0) The Fool
1) The Magician
2) The High Priestess
3) The Empress
4) The Emperor
5) The Hierophant

TAROT FOR BEGINNERS

6) The Lovers
7) The Chariot
8) Justice
9) The Hermit
10) Wheel of Fortune
11) Strength
12) The Hanged Man
13) Death
14) Temperance
15) The Devil
16) The Tower
17) The Star
18) The Moon
19) The Sun
20) Judgment
21) The World

The Cards of the Major Arcana: Meanings

0 - The Fool: The fool starts the deck, and in a lot of ways, this is reflective of the card reader. If you have ever heard of "the fool's journey," then you may know that the tarot deck is often considered to be this card's stroll through life. The fool is number zero, and so he is outside of the tarot deck, numerically, the same way that the reader is. The fool is thought to be vulnerable, as they have yet to encounter just how tough life is. But since they have not yet been tested by life, there is the opportunity for them to show great strength to rise above the hardships. But the fool can also be overwhelmed. Some seem to think, based on the name, that the fool represents stupidity or mistakes in some way. The fool is not a moron; he merely lacks life experience. When the fool is pulled, you want to align with him to take on the challenges of life with the fool's open eagerness.

1 - The Magician: The magician isn't an outside force that one encounters. For example, as the fool, you don't then meet the magician. The magician is something that is inside the reader or the person receiving the tarot reading. The magician card is meant to remind us that we are all magical in our own way. This may actually be the case with someone with magical talent, but it is also a metaphoric reading. For example, a talented musician has magic in the form of the skills they have honed over a lifetime at their craft. The magician reminds us that we are powerful but also unique, that the powers we hold are ours and ours alone. If the magician is revealed then you should take action, he reminds us that the time to act is now because we have the skills to get the job done, or the ability to learn them if we set ourselves to it. This doesn't mean that you should rush every time you see the magician. Sometimes it can be a reminder of the skills you have, a reminder to look for a better solution to your problem that is more in tune to your frequencies rather than what you're trying currently. Whether the magician is telling you to rush or wait will depend on the question and your interpretation.

2 - The High Priestess: The high priestess represents your consciousness, both the part you are aware of and the subconscious part that happens without your knowledge. Like the magician, the high priestess tells us to look inside of ourselves for the answer. The magician points us towards our skills, but the high priestess guides us towards what we feel in our guts. The high priestess is a reminder that our instincts are to be trusted, and that we have gained these innate feelings and instincts for a reason. When she shows herself in a reading, she tells us to look here, to this source of knowledge inside of ourselves, for the answer. But, just because the knowledge is inside of us, that doesn't mean it is always easy. Sometimes the knowledge that the priestess tells us to seek is that which makes us feel the most vulnerable or scared. The high priestess does not represent good or bad, but rather points us towards where we should be looking for our answers.

3 - The Empress: The empress is also sometimes thought of as the mother due to her deep-rooted ties to mother nature. But the empress is not mother nature;

she is simply linked to mother nature through her connection to beauty and love. The empress sees mother nature as something to love, as much as she loves those around her and her own existence. The empress is feminine, through and through, and this can be a reminder for us to get back in touch with that feminine part of ourselves. This applies to men as much as women. Her connection to mother nature reminds us to stop and smell the roses. She can be a sign that we have fallen out of touch with the world around us or the love we have inside. She is also a reminder that true beauty and happiness don't need to come from wealth, but from love and empathy. She is said to be a very potent card, and her presence can completely change the way you approach your question in the future.

4 - The Emperor: An emperor has to be a man of power, a man of force. An emperor has to be able to rally troops to his cause and keep men working under him honestly so that the needs of the empire are thought of above the selfishness of men. So it makes perfect sense that the emperor card represents our own leadership and power. But if you aren't naturally a leader of men, then you might not think that you have any leadership skills. You'd be wrong. The emperor card reminds us that we are the emperor of our own lives, and our choices are what lead us through life. If we keep making poor decisions, then we aren't demonstrating ourselves to be very capable emperors. But when we take control of our lives and remember this part of ourselves, we can step into the present and keep our empire healthy, safe, and secure. When we become aware of our strength, we not only become aware of how we are using it but also the effect it has on others. This brings our awareness to the fact that our actions don't happen in a vacuum, but affect those around us. Poor decisions can lead to the people around us hurting, yet, with a little bit of leadership, we can bring positivity to the situation.

5 - The Hierophant: The hierophant card represents our connection to our spirituality. The hierophant is a card that represents a connection to the divine. That doesn't mean that the card itself has a connection, but rather, it reminds us to take a step back from our problem, our question, and think about it from our unique spiritual perspective. There are many problems we encounter, which cause us to get lost in the world of logic or details. We lose sight of how we feel about the problem on a spiritual level. Sometimes, we need to do what we feel and leave a project behind or remove a harmful influence from our lives. Sometimes we need to stop thinking about how we can profit, and start thinking about how we can help one another. Whatever the question is, the hierophant reminds us that answers can be found in that intangible and personal spiritual realm that is inside each one of us.

6 - The Lovers: The lovers is a favorite card of lots of people. Artwork for the lovers has been featured in many shows, movies, video games, and album covers. It is probably the third most recognizable card after death and the fool. The lovers is accurately titled, as its purpose is to bring out awareness back to our love life. Perhaps we have gotten a little bit lost in a particular problem and didn't even realize that our love life was suffering. Or maybe we've been stagnant so long, and this is a sign of something on the imminent horizon. While the lovers is most often represented in this fashion, we should keep in mind the metaphoric value of the tarot deck. The lovers can also be seen as simply a representation of something you love. The particular question you asked will make the lovers' role more apparent. If you are consulting with the tarot deck because you are unsure of where you want to go in life, the lovers are a little more ominous. They remind us to consider our choice carefully because our actions have consequences on those we love, and we may not have identified all of the possible issues yet.

7 - The Chariot: The chariot represents that engine inside each of us. We all have an inner drive that pushes us to work harder at what we love. It's why we push ourselves in the gym or on the sports field. It's why a writer tries to squeeze a page in during their coffee break, or why a doctor keeps up with the latest medical discoveries. We all have a drive inside of us, and the chariot card reminds us not to forget about this. The stress of life can weigh us down and make us lose sight of our drive. Sometimes we are distracted by too much work, and that drive starts to fade away. The chariot card reminds us that stoking that fire is the only way to keep the engine going, but that once it is working, there is no stopping where you can get to. The chariot is a formidable card that suggests great things are on the horizon so long as you grit your teeth and keep the fire burning.

8 - Justice: Depending on which deck you are using, #8 and #11 may have their places swapped. We step outside of ourselves when we consider justice. This is not a card that tells us to look inside of us or to consider personal knowledge. Instead, justice is the hard truth of the world. It is a law that none of us can escape. When the justice card comes up, we're not talking about the kind of justice the police represent. The justice card is about karma, that universal justice that might not always be visible. It's that justice that sees bad men punished for their Faustian deals and good men venerated. Justice can be read as a harsh reminder that your circumstances are the result of your deeds. Your actions are the reason for your problems. Of course, this also means that anything positive you are experiencing is also because of your own doing. Justice is impartial when it comes to your reasons or your experience; it is just a force in the universe. However, if justice comes up, then you should take it as a reminder to be on your best behavior and not to hurt those around you.

9 - The Hermit: The hermit is another reminder that the answers we are looking for are already inside of us. That is, if the hermit comes up alone as the source of the answer, then we know that we have to look inside of us. The hermit also modifies other cards. For example, the emperor points us towards the power that we are bringing, and this isn't necessarily inside of us as much as it is something we control and use at all times. The hermit doesn't steer us away from the emperor, but he gives us a sign of the best tool to use to get at the knowledge. The hermit likes to spend time alone, his quiet, his peace. He wants to be away from people, away from noise, away from distraction. The hermit card tells us to reflect on the problem that we are facing. With the emperor card, this might mean that we should meditate and consider the way that we are using our power and whether it is helping or hurting our cause. Sometimes we get so lost in everything that we don't realize we've been surrounding ourselves with outside influence and forgotten to listen to our inner voices. The hermit is a sign that it is time for us to return to ourselves.

10 - Wheel of Fortune: No, this card isn't a sign that you're about to be a contestant on your favorite game show. Instead of the bright lights of the spinning wheel from TV, the wheel of fortune card is better thought of as a clock that we are all hanging from. We're stuck on the hands of the clock as they spin around endlessly. This is a good reminder that time takes all things from us, that the natural state of existence is change. However, the wheel is not the wheel of time, but the wheel of fortune, and this implies another truth for us to grasp. When it comes to our good fortune, it comes and it goes. Sometimes we have it, and we're on top of the world; other times, it is nowhere to be seen, and we feel like we're hanging on for dear life. The wheel of fortune reminds us that we will lose everything that we have or ever gain. There is no permanence. Some find this horribly depressing, but it is meant as a reminder to cherish the good while it is here but to be ready to accept when it is gone rather than mourn. In a spread, it reminds us that the good is temporary, but the bad is transient as well. It may be a sign that change is coming soon, or that you need to take a moment to enjoy the present. Regardless of whether it comes up in a spread or not, the wheel of fortune will continue to turn.

11 - Strength: Depending on which deck you are using, #8 and #11 may have their places swapped. The strength card isn't about how well you do at the test-your-strength game at the carnival; it's about how well you do going through the haunted house. This card is about your courage in the face of hurt and danger, and your ability to weather the struggles that life throws at all of us. No matter how low or useless or powerless you have felt, if you are reading this book, then you are still alive, and that means that you have strength inside you that you continue to tap into every day. When you feel the lowest is when you use the most strength. Depression and anxiety can be massive burdens, but if you're facing life with them and continuing to get out of bed each day, then you are demonstrating massive amounts of strength. This card reminds you of this, this forgotten strength, so that you can remember just how powerful you are. It reminds us that we have faced troubles, problems, and crises in our lives, and so this current one is fully within our capabilities to master.

12 - The Hanged Man: The hanged man is a confused character. He's often depicted as not only hanging but hanging upside down. Sometimes when you draw him, you will instinctively place him upside down because he looks like he should be standing normally. This confusing quality is wonderfully fitting as the hanged man is a sign that you are confused. You are in a liminal space between where you're coming from, and where you want to go, but you aren't sure exactly what to do. When you're confused like this, you are left feeling like you are hanging. You need to find the nail that has you trapped so that you can get out. This could be an old way of thinking, a bad habit, your credit card debt, or a thousand other things. Something has you caught up, and you need to let it go so that you can turn the world right-side up and find where you are supposed to be going again. Remember that the hanged man often has to give up something to get out. He's hanging by a nail through his clothes, so they're likely to get ripped. Getting hung up on something often results in us having to give that thing up. It might be comfortable to keep texting an ex-partner, but if you're still hung up in the past, then you can't move forward. The things we give up might be enjoyable, but if they're getting in your way, then you can't move on with them weighing you down.

13 - Death: Death is the most widely known card. As we talked about in chapter one, drawing the death card does not mean that you are going to die. Reading tarot cards is reading the intentions and meaning of the cards and how they interact with each other. If the death card comes up, then its interpretation is going to be determined by which slot it came up in. Movies like to have it come up in the future slot so that characters get a nice scare before the real action of the story starts. In reality, this would be more likely to tell you that one phase of your life is about to end, and another is about to commence. The death card is about the end of things like behaviors, influences, relationships, careers, projects, problems. The death of something good means the end of its influence in your life. This is a sad thing, but where one thing ends, something new can begin, and this can be a source of the most wonderful joy. The death card could also be thought of as the "change" card because that is what it ultimately signals.

14 - Temperance: The temperance card is like the hermit in that it is not about an answer inside of us, but about how we should go about getting to the answer. The hermit tells us that we need to seek our solitude to mull it over in silence. Temperance, on the other hand, reminds us that we need to be patient without getting upset. The temperance card finds a lot of parallels in the values of Buddhism, as it tells us we need to allow ourselves to accept that life happens in a manner that we cannot predict. Things come and things go, things change. We make plans, and then suddenly, something comes up. All of these can be frustrating, but we can choose to accept them and let them go, or we can choose to get upset. The temperance card is a reminder that this is the natural state of existence, and there is no reason to get upset about it. Instead, remember to go with the flow. Do your best, but don't get upset when things alter. Change is the natural state of all things, and life is wildly unpredictable. If you see temperance, remember this and consider how you can loosen your hold on any certainties you still have about the future.

15 - The Devil: The devil card is almost certainly the reason that some people still call tarot cards, "the devil's picture book," but it isn't about demons or the devil in a Biblical sense. Again, we're working with metaphors here. There are a lot of times in life when we feel powerless as if life is out of our control, and there is nothing we can do about it. It is in times like these that the devil is likely to appear. The devil is not only drawn by these feelings; he's the cause of them. The devil card represents the ways that we trick ourselves into thinking we are powerless. We do this all the time. In neuroscience terms, we continually reinforce negative thoughts, which create lasting impacts on the physical structure of the brain through neuroplasticity. The devil card represents these and reminds us of them. It means we have become trapped. We've forgotten that we are the source of our power and that everything inside us is under our control. The devil obscures us from seeing that we are emperors and tricks us into sabotaging our own lives. When the devil comes up, take it as a sign that there is a negative influence blocking your full potential. Look for the way to remove the devil's influence so that you can reconnect with your inner emperor and regain authority over your life.

16 - The Tower: While Christians are most disturbed by the devil card, and people fed on movies and television are scared of the death card, tarot readers hope to avoid the tower more than any other card. The tower is destruction, and it is often depicted as a burning wreck of a building. The problem with the tower is that when it comes up, we will naturally want to avoid it. That is especially true if we are doing a reading for somebody else. Nobody wants to hear about this, and others aren't educated enough in tarot to realize that it is already too late. When the tower comes up, there is only one thing left to do. It simply burns. You can't save it; you can only wait for the flames to go out so you can start to build something new. Like the devil card, the tower card comes up most often when there are feelings of hopelessness. Crumbling marriages and careers bring the tower card out to play in a hurry. It represents a painful experience, but it leaves behind fertile soil for the future's growth.

17 - The Star: The star is the polar opposite of the tower. Rather than destruction and pain, the star is a sign that healing is on the way. The star reminds us not to give up hope, and that good things are coming. Health, happiness, and good times. For artists, it means a muse is coming. For depression, it means that help is on the way if you look for it. If the tower is about the possibility of fertile soil, then the star is about planting new roots in that soil and beginning a new future. While there is no direct good luck charm in the tarot deck, the star is the closest version of it because it suggests the brightness of a new day. This is especially welcome after a long storm or the time spent burning the tower.

18 - The Moon: The moon card is one that can change its meaning greatly depending on where it is placed. In general, the moon is your subconscious, kind of like the high priestess. But where the high priestess is about consciousness itself, the moon is more about the contents of the subconscious. This means every thought you didn't realize you had and every feeling you haven't addressed is a part of the moon card. Every doubt you've never vocalized, and every fear that has driven or crippled you, all of these falls under the moon card as well. With such a wide range of areas which the moon card could represent, the spread itself is going to be important to determine which is the most appropriate. When it is pulled, the moon is often a sign that the contents of your subconscious are out of alignment. This may be the cause of anxiety and worry. We have a problem in which our subconscious takes on a lot more information than we realize, mostly due to how much time we spend watching TV or scrolling through social media. These things aren't necessarily bad in any way, but the moon card tells us that it might be time to look at the contents of the subconscious to let go of a lot of it. Fears, anxieties, stressors, misguided beliefs, anything that you didn't realize was weighing you down can be let go.

19 - The Sun: The sun is like the star in that is another card that is wonderful to see in a reading. The star offered hope because new things were coming soon, the sun informs us that we are moving in the right direction and that we should continue doing what we are doing because it will shortly be paying off for us. The sun also suggests to us that there is a lot of happiness around us, as happiness and success seem to come hand in hand. Where there is happiness, success catches up; success doesn't bring happiness, but it likes to follow behind. The sun tells us there is happiness around us and that we should appreciate what is happening and the people we know. Often, when we do this, we find that it is these same people that we appreciate that bring us the best opportunities and chances to grow. Remember that when the sun shines, things are bright, and you are making progress along the right path.

20 - Judgment: The judgment card is a call to stop and stare long and hard at your life and how it has been going. When it comes up in a reading, this card reminds us that we are working towards a future and what the future is can change at any moment. If you want to work in movies but ended up in TV because you thought it was your way in, it is more than okay to change your goal to something related to this new circumstance. You can aim for whatever kind of future you want; it is entirely up to you at any moment. You are the emperor of your own life, you get to decide. Because of this, you also know that you can change and leave your past self behind. That doesn't need to continue existing and holding you down. These are powerful reminders that will help greatly. When you see the judgment card, you should take some time to reflect on where you have come from and where you are now. Then consider where you want to be. How far have you come, and what do you need to do to get there? Is it still something you want, or is it time to set a new future? All of these are under your control, and the judgment card reminds us to recalibrate these values so we can get a better understanding of who we are and live more fully in line with our values.

21 - The World: The world represents everything, and this means the end of the fool's journey; every desire has been achieved. Each part of the tarot deck so far has either been about a part of you or the way that events are going to play out. The world represents you as each of these parts combined into a single whole. You are every other card and the lessons they hold, now in a single card. When the world is drawn, you know that you are doing well and that the road you are walking is leading you directly to your unique destiny as a complete individual. However, as wonderful as this is, it needs to be remembered that this is referring to the question being asked of the tarot cards and not just life as a whole. So, the world points towards the answer, the positive outcome, the resolution of an issue. Whether it ends poorly or well, it ended the way it needed to end for you to continue on the path you are on. The world is a treasured card because it comes at the end of the deck. The deck doesn't end on a downer. Life is an extraordinary thing according to the fool's journey, and there are hard lessons to be learned, but they're what gives us greater power over our lives, and this is a truly excellent way to end the major arcana.

The Cards of the Minor Arcana: Introduction

There are 56 cards in minor arcana, which means that there is a lot to cover. Thankfully, it is divided into four suits, and each suit is made up of the same cards. It's like a suit from a deck of playing cards, only there is one more card between the 10 and the jack. We'll take a quick glance at how this looks and then go through each of the suits individually.

The Cards of the Minor Arcana: At a Glance

Suits
Wands
Cups
Swords
Coin

Cards
Ace
Two
Three
Four
Five
Six
Seven
Eight
Nine
Ten
Page
Knight
Queen
King

The Cards of the Minor Arcana: The Meaning of Wands

Wands: Wands have connections to clubs, fire, and artisans, but in their use relating purely to the tarot, they are more in line with creativity and engineering. Clever business ideas and new creative projects are all the tone of wands. But, rather than getting an idea and letting it go, wands are about action and taking risks in the name of dreams and ambitions. Wands are all about thinking of something new and then going out and doing it because without action, there is no reaction, and ideas don't have any power on their own. If you get a wand in a reading, then you need to be putting something into action soon.

Ace: The ace of wands is the first card in this suit, and so it represents the beginning of a journey, its creative and innovative aspects. The ace of wands is the first step of the new project, the idea percolating in the brain or being shared with friends. When you see the ace, keep an eye out for the project that needs to begin.

Two: Fittingly, two of wands is that second step where you go from talking and start doing. It's where you learn new ideas and test them out rather than sit at home and dream about them. When you see the two, you know it is time to run in this new direction with everything you've got.

Three: This is that feeling of joy and hope you get when you are just starting a new project. Creatives like writers love this part of a new project because it is the most exciting time, and the ideas are fresh. This reminds us that the best ideas and chances come when we open ourselves up to our creativity. If we aren't prepared to act on new endeavors, then we lose this hope, but we can always regain it.

Four: The four of wands reminds us that solid plans require reliable builders and that this often comes in the form of other people. We frequently may try to do everything ourselves, especially in the competitiveness of today's modern job market. But oftentimes, the most powerful and influential forces come from groups of people rather than any one person acting alone. Look towards the people around you that you can count on when you see this one.

Five: The five of wands shows up when there is stiff competition. This might be because you are planning to make big moves or because you have a strong opponent in your way. It is important to remember that winning is one thing, but being mean will only cause harm to those around you. The five of wands tells us to slow down for a moment, to consider who might get hurt as a result of this competition, and to consider if that is worth it.

Six: The six of wands is all about what we are getting back for our hard work. If we keep going and doing our best and continually pushing forward, we will be celebrated and respected for what we have achieved. Getting a six of wands does not mean that you are ready to stop, but rather that you are going in the right direction, and people are recognizing how much you are doing. Drawing this card reminds us to be pleased with what we've done and to accept praise with an open heart.

Seven: This card represents a happy person, content with their work. This can be a tremendous indication that we are on the right path, but this card, in particular, warns us about not getting too comfortable where we are. Change is the state of existence, and we need to be aware of where we are and ready to react to changing circumstances as they arise. Drawing a seven of wands isn't a sign that you should stop being happy but simply that you must keep working if you want everything to continue working out.

Eight: Drawing the eight of wands reminds us that everything can happen in a moment's notice. Things go fast in the real world, and sometimes we can't keep up with all the changes. But change is the natural state of things, and so we must do our best, and find new ways through them.

Nine: No matter how hard a worker you are, you are going to need to rest sometimes. If you are like me, then you're a workaholic who doesn't sleep nearly enough, so remember to take notice whenever you draw the nine of wands. This card tells us that we need to rest, to heal either physically, mentally, or emotionally. We might be working ourselves to the bone looking for a solution to a problem, and we forget to sleep. Our productivity levels are down, and we're only further away from an answer than we would be otherwise. Take time to rest when you see the nine of wands.

Ten: The ten of wands is the opposite of the nine. The nine tells us we need to rest; the ten tells us there is no time to rest! Sometimes we get into situations where the only way out of them is to keep going as hard as we can. When this is the case, you're likely to find the ten of wands popping up in your readings.

Page: This is a very interesting card. The page is an innovative fellow who doesn't care what other people think about him. In the case of the page of wands, he wants to be free to create and carry out any weird project that comes to mind. The page's goal is a liberation of the self into pure creative investigation. That takes a lot of love and passion and desire, and it can become the source of tremendous power. We all have a page inside, but we have a hard time getting to them. When you see the page of wands in your readings, dig deep and look for that ray of light that catches your interest and brings a new meaning to your reality.

Knight: The knight of wands has a big problem. He is quick to attack the people around him rather than wait to learn their intentions. He acts fast, but that action is never well thought out. The knight acts without fear; he goes after what he wants and has no concern for what happens because of it. Drawing a knight of wands doesn't necessarily mean this is bad, but it might be a warning that you need to rein in that side of yourself so that you can get back in touch with your intelligence to plan appropriately.

Queen: The queen of wands is a formidable card. The queen acts, rather than talks or dreams. She is full of energy that leaks out to those around her and feeds them. When she brings her positive energy, this has an invigorating effect. The queen of wands is a kind-hearted character, but one that demands actions. This means that she represents a struggle to be engaged in, but she does so as a motivator. When you draw her, be proud of how you act and respect yourself when interacting with the people around you.

King: The king of wands is not just a leader, but a hero. He is a CEO, a film director, the head of a company, or the manager of any number of teams. The king of wands went out, and he made something of himself. But he doesn't stop there. The king of wands can't stop, adventure calls his name, and the only thing he knows for sure is that there is more he wants to see. He likes his position, it brings him lots of joy, and if he is wise, then he shares that joy with those around him. When you draw the king of wands, take a moment to revel in your power and how important you are. Then, once you appreciate yourself, you can turn it outwards to continue being a true hero.

The Cards of the Minor Arcana: The Meaning of Cups

Cups: In tarot, the suit of cups is most closely connected to the spirit inside each of us. This spirit is created in our connections to ourselves and our emotions, as well as to the feelings and lives of the people around us. Cups point us towards matters of the heart and soul, sometimes even the ethereal realm of dreams. These cards are connected to water and warm weather, like a beach in the summer. They invite you to dive into the water to cool off from the hot rays of the sun. They're also there for those dark nights when you want to walk alongside the shoreline and consider what you feel to be true in your heart.

Ace: We get tight and worried and lost in our fears and emotions. The ace of cups is aware of this and understands that we need a healing balm from time to time. When you draw the ace of cups, take a moment to drink from its healing waters by spending time with those you love and sharing interests and emotions freely with one another.

Two: Everyone wants the two to come up in love spreads because it represents soul mates. Of course, it doesn't need to be a romantic partner; it can be a mentor or teacher or even a good friend or a business partner. Anyone that you meld with in a strong way can fit with this cup. When you draw it, invest more time and attention into that relationship so that it remains fruitful.

Three: While the two of cups is about tight bonds with partners, the three of cups reminds us to take time to invest in our relationships with those around us who help us in our work and lives. Babysitters, co-workers, friends, family, grocery store employees, and baristas are just some of the many people that you might consider honoring. Reach out to these people and let them know that you understand how they are helping you, and you appreciate it.

Four: The four of cups is about getting stuck. You don't know where you are anymore or what you are supposed to be doing, and you just feel plain old stuck with nowhere to go. When you feel like this, you can get lost in anxiety and negativity and miss the way out that's right in front of you. This card is a warning not to get lost in our negativity.

Five: The five of cups represents a period of emotional struggle and pain. It is a time in which you are overwhelmed with sadness, or you are lost in regrets over something that you've done in the past. Maybe you didn't get a promotion, or you regret breaking up with your boyfriend. Whatever the case, we all go through these periods. The five of cups is a sign that we need to forgive ourselves and let go of the past. We must focus on the future.

Six: There is a lot of wonder and amazement in the world when seen through the eyes of a child. Everything holds such hope and promise, and there are endless possibilities. Then, as we get older, we seem to lose touch with this wonder and these possibilities. We close ourselves up to all the beauty and mini-miracles that happen around us every day. The six of cups is a sign that we need to get back in touch with this freshness and look at the world with new eyes.

Seven: The seven of cups represents the imagination. This might be an imagination with lots of wonderment, as discussed with the six of cups, but it could be a boring place if you haven't used it very much. Whatever it is, your imagination is yours to control, and with it, you can pick what your future is going to be. You can also choose what to make of the present moment, free to change your mind or stay in character. Drawing the seven of cups can let us know that we haven't enough imagination in our lives and we need more. It can also warn us when we've become lost in that imagination, and we've stopped seeing the real picture. Either way, we either have too little or too much when this card comes up.

Eight: The eight of cups is an unfortunate card to draw because it represents disappointment. Since we're talking about cups and they deal in that emotional space, this is often something like a broken heart, a mistrustful friend, or a disappointing experience. The eight of cups often appears near the end of a problem, when there is little left you can do, but accept there is pain you must deal with. When things don't work out, and you feel let down, the eight of cups comes to remind us that it is okay to be upset, but we can take that energy and put it elsewhere so that we stay productive rather than destructive.

Nine: The opposite of the eight of cups, the nine of cups shows up when things are working out, or soon will do. It is one of those cards that everybody wants in their reading because it is considered to bring good luck.

When you see it, there is nothing that you need to do. Just continue focusing on the good side of life and working hard at what you love without hurting others. It is all about to pay off now.

Ten: Another card that everyone likes to get, the ten of cups is a sign that it's time to celebrate and take stock of those you love. The ten of cups means that everywhere you look, there is love looking back at you. You have put out so much love that it now greets you wherever you go, and you have nothing to worry about. When you see the ten of cups, you can rest easy knowing that you are making tremendous progress through life and that the people around you want nothing but the best for you.

Page: The page of cups is a fascinating card. They are emotionally vulnerable and could easily be hurt if they aren't careful. They believe strongly in their ideals, and they have powerful imaginations. This can help them to seek considerable success in life and much happiness in their spirits, but they are also open to deep pain if they don't respond to the world properly. The page of cups needs to learn to protect themselves without losing touch with the youthful spirit that drives them. If you draw the page of cups, you should remember to be more like the page and open yourself up. Take risks like a child, and be ready to learn to protect yourself without losing yourself.

Knight: The knight of cups is a hero that everyone can love. He is wise and knows much about love while also being deeply intelligent about many subjects. People find the knight of cups to be charming, and he creates a seductive air without even trying. But he does this because more than anything, he is a man of action. When the knight of cups dreams up an adventure, he immediately sets forth on it. He gets beat up and takes his share of tumbles, but he always finds his way to glory in the end. If you draw the knight of cups, then take comfort knowing that you are on a brave and exciting path, and the struggles you face will end with much to take pride in.

Queen: The queen of cups is another card that is representative of our inner female and the connection we have to our emotions. The queen of cups represents love and understanding, given freely to the whole of existence rather than conditioned and given only to those that please her the most. She feels deeply and understands that emotions are fleeting experiences to be treasured, whether they be good or bad. If you draw the queen of cups, then you need to take some time and get back in touch with those feelings deep inside. Remember, too, to act like the queen of cups does, and open your heart to the world around you and from a place of love rather than negativity or spitefulness.

King: The king of cups is an impressive card. So much so that the king sits and never speaks, he radiates his authority and control. People know not to mess with the king of cups because his power is a deep one, one that doesn't require him to be flashy or show it off. It is a force to be afraid of, but not a force that he uses for fear. The king of cups has risen above being controlled by his emotions, and he doesn't use emotions to control others. He understands that feelings tell him more about himself and what he knows to be right, and this space between feeling and acting gives him great power. When you draw the king of cups, look deep inside yourself. Look at the scariest of all of your emotions, but do so with the calmness of a king. See what your deepest and most raw emotions are, and then take control of them so that you can live like the king of cups does.

The Cards of the Minor Arcana: The Meaning of Swords

Swords: It probably comes as no surprise that the suit most aligned to hardship and struggle is swords. After all, the sword has been the cause of and the settler of countless struggles throughout history. These cards come up most often when there are hardships in your life that you need to overcome. The theme of swords ranges much wider than the other suits, and it covers issues ranging from anger to death and destruction, as well as loss and sorrow. They are thought of as being attuned to the autumn season and the air. Some believe that when swords show up, they help to sharpen a person's awareness and help them cut to the truth of their problems.

Ace: The ace of swords is a connection to the motivating force that pushes you forward through life. This sword is one that represents hope and a chance at success. It often appears when you are starting a new project or escaping from another. If you draw it, then you should remember that you have the strength to take on the challenges ahead. Always hope for the best, not dread and fear the worst.

Two: This card represents the need to make a decision. If you draw it, then remember that the two of swords is misunderstood. People most commonly think that the two of swords means that you have to make a decision now. But this card is patient and understands the value in gathering information before acting.

Three: Lovers all across the world dread this card. It represents heartbreak and the pain of losing someone dear to us. Drawing the three of swords might mean that you are going to have to face sadness in the near future, though it often shows itself when you are already going through your pain. When you see this card, you may want to run from everything that you are doing, but it is telling you to accept it and let the pain come. It will leave soon, and you will be stronger for it.

Four: The four of swords represents rest, and it reminds us that we need to take the time to rest if we want to keep producing, succeeding, or winning at the goals we set. When you draw the four of swords, it means that it's time to take a vacation, catch up on rest, and get back in touch with that quiet place inside yourself.

Five: Conflict brings tension, and the five of swords understands this well. This card reminds us that every fight we have comes at a cost. We don't only lose when we fail, but we also lose when our success costs us something near and dear. Winning an argument doesn't help if you insulted the other person to do it. When you draw this card, you should stop and consider if the cost of your success is damaging those around you.

Six: This card represents leaving behind a painful or harmful situation. Sometimes the only answer we have is to turn around and walk away. We can't beat every challenge, after all. It might fill us with fear, regret, or sadness when we walk away, but it is necessary, so remember this when you draw this card.

Seven: Deception is a part of the world around us. It doesn't necessarily have to be a bad thing, though we often consider it as such. The seven of swords is our connection to that deception, and drawing it tells us that we need to consider if there is a deception that we have fallen for.

Eight: Sometimes, there is nothing to do but weather the storm. We can't find shelter around us, and so we need to keep going through an uncomfortable experience until we can finally do something to make it better. That can be a hurtful thing to accept, but once we understand this, we can keep walking forward without letting it get us down. This card reminds us that we have to let go of our constant need to be free. Once we do, we find that the chains that bound us weren't so tight after all.

Nine: We face anxiety all the time. We're afraid of failure, of success, of losing, of winning. We often lose ourselves to these fears, and they can make us feel like we don't matter. The nine of swords reminds us that these feelings come and go and that we don't need to let them continue to upset us.

Ten: The ten of swords represents the end, the breaking point, the moment where there is no way to retreat, no way back. This might mean the end of a relationship, issues with money, or words that can't be unsaid. When you see the ten of swords, remember that you can't go back and so you shouldn't let the past hold you down. Focus on moving forward instead.

Page: The page of swords is a character of action. This page is always in motion, ready to move with a smile on his face. He has access to all of the knowledge he needs to find success, and so the page of swords understands that he has to act to actualize it. When you draw the page of swords, remind yourself to act as he does.

Knight: The knight of swords is like the page of swords but even more ready for action. He isn't afraid of anything, knowing he is armored in his will power and mental strength. The knight of swords tells us it is time to push ourselves forward with more gusto.

Queen: The queen of swords is a decisive lady that understands what she wants out of life. She doesn't need to lie or cheat her way to it; instead, she chooses honesty and kindness. Such behavior never comes at the cost of her independence, as she has no interest in the whims of others. Drawing the queen of swords is a reminder to be true to ourselves and not what others want us to be.

King: The king of swords is a symbol of wisdom. He is free from the struggles of emotion, and looks at the world with logic and the knowledge of a wizened hero. He may be considered cold, but he doesn't try to be; he is merely confident and secure in himself. When you draw him, he reminds us of this strength inside of ourselves and how we can use it to lead and guide others.

The Cards of the Minor Arcana: The Meaning of Coins

Coins: Coins are often referred to as pentacles. Either label works well for them, as this suit is most concerned with material objects and the physical world. Materials may be actual coins, as in the case of wealth, or they may be objects and items purchased and obtained throughout life. Some consider our love for material objects to be a rein that holds us back, and thus pentacles serves as an apt descriptor in the place of coins. This suit is most tightly related to the winter and the element of earth. Drawing a coin is a sign that there is something that needs your attention, not inside of yourself but in the world outside. Listen to the cards to use your attention wisely.

Ace: As with all aces, the ace of coins represents a beginning as well. That is the beginning of the life that you have worked hard to gain and achieve. These will be your first steps, and you mustn't forget them. If you draw the ace of coins, seek support, and prepare to push forward.

Two: The two of coins represents a change coming. Like the wheel of fortune, the two of coins show us that success and failure are linked, and that one being up means the other is down, but they're always coming back around. If you draw this card, then realize that change is coming, and it can't be stopped.

Three: This card represents intelligence of the highest form. A triumph of genius is in the works, but it needs time for it to come together. When you draw this card, you should know that you are doing well, but you should never forget to plan, consider, and contemplate your actions with intelligence rather than act from a place of ignorance or rashness.

Four: This card represents the fact that all material goods we acquire will fade and go away in time. Possibly that's a scary experience for many to face, but remembering that what comes also goes can be quite good for us. When we draw this card, we shouldn't forget that our material wealth will fade if we aren't careful, and so we should take measures to protect ourselves and our possessions.

Five: This card represents the ideas of desire and of being grateful for what we have. Getting something that we desire fills us with a sense of gratitude, but also one that fades in time. Drawing this card reminds us that while we are happy with money and material goods, we shouldn't confuse this happiness with real, deep-seated happiness.

Six: This card represents generosity, though generosity that comes at a price. This card tells us that getting and giving are not separate events, but two parts of the same coin. When you give, you receive. When you take, you lose. Drawing the six of coins is a sign that you must show and share with others.

Seven: This is another card that reminds us that hard work is required if we want to profit. We like to look for an easy route through struggles and hardships, but the truth of the matter is that we need to work hard. Drawing this card reminds us that it's this labor that will bring us our successes.

Eight: This card is used to represent improvement. If you draw the eight of coins, then you know that you need to continue working on yourself, your skills, your relationships, or whatever else that position of the spread was related to.

Nine: Dealing with material goods, it is no surprise that the nine of coins is all about financial security. We all want to have money without worries or fears, and that is what this card represents. Drawing it points you towards the work that needs to be done to find this security in your life.

Ten: The ten of coins represents the results of all that hard work. The wealth, respect, and pleasures that we achieve from our hard work are all included in this card, and drawing it is a reminder that your goals don't happen overnight. You will need to put the time in to actualize them.

Page: Young and ready to tackle the world, the page of coins believes he has everything he could ever want. The page of coins knows he can take his winnings and double them, and he can meet any challenge. But he does this because he seeks knowledge and understanding. When you draw him, slow down your plans and seek your own knowledge.

Knight: This knight is the most peaceful of the four suits, as he spends his time worrying about growth rather than action. This knight knows that skills grow on top of each other, that relationships grow, and that plans and actions have wide-ranging consequences that develop with time. Drawing him is a reminder to look at how these actions ripple out and affect the whole.

Queen: The queen of coins loves to solve problems, and drawing her is a sign that you can find answers to your difficulties in her peace and her goodwill.

King: The king of coins has lots of material and spiritual wealth to show the world. He has followed the path of the coins and has acquired more than he could have ever dreamed of. This brings influence and respect, but the king of coins knows that to keep power, you must be careful with it. Drawing the king of coins should serve as a reminder to keep working and to walk the path of strength and respect.

TAROT FOR BEGINNERS

Chapter Summary

- There are 78 cards in a deck of tarot cards. 22 of these are in the major arcana, and 56 of them are in the minor arcana.

- The major arcana are numbered 0-21.

- The fool represents the start of the journey that is the tarot cards, and so the major arcana are sometimes known as the fool's journey.

- The magician represents that special skill that is inside all of us.

- The high priest is our consciousness.

- The empress is connected to mother nature and love.

- The emperor rules over his empire much as we rule over life.

- The hierophant is our connection to our spirituality.

- The lovers are all about connection.

- The chariot is the engine of motivation inside of us.

- Justice is universal justice on a cosmic level.

TAROT FOR BEGINNERS

- The hermit reminds us to seek solitude to answer questions.

- The wheel of fortune continues to turn, just like our fortunes come and go.

- Strength reminds us that we have the power to push through hardship and keep going.

- The hanged man tells us we need to set ourselves right, and that doing so often comes at a cost.

- Death is a reminder that all things end, but that where one thing ends, another can start.

- Temperance reminds us we need to be patient to get to the answer.

- The devil represents the ways we get trapped inside ourselves.

- The tower is a sad card because it represents a burning structure, project, or relationship that can't be fixed.

- The star represents hope and new beginnings.

- The moon is the subconscious.

- The sun tells us to keep going in the same direction.

- Judgment reminds us there is a cosmic karma.

- The world is the end of the tarot deck, and represents the coming together of all the lessons of the tarot into one actualized person.

- There are four suits of the minor arcana: wands, cups, swords, and coins.

- Each suit has an ace, two, three, four, five, six, seven, eight, nine, ten, page, knight, queen, and king.

- The wand suit is related to fire, artisans, creativity, and engineering. The cards in this deck are mostly related to creativity and how it helps us to overcome challenges.

- The cup suit is connected to the spirit inside of us all and helps us gain understanding of questions of the heart and emotions.

- The sword suit is about getting through hardship and dealing with struggle; it points us towards ways that we can fix our problems.

- The coin suit is related to material goods. Drawing cards from it points us towards answers in the realm of the physical, outer world.

In the next chapter, you will learn a few of the most common spreads from three-card spreads that can be used for almost anything, and complex spreads to answer questions of the heart and the career.

CHAPTER FIVE

COMMON TAROT SPREADS

Now that you know what the cards mean, you can start to lay them down and read them correctly. You can always do an intuitive reading and let the cards guide you, but 90% of the time that tarot cards are used, they're done in a spread. There are thousands of spreads that you can discover and learn to use. If you can't find one that works for you, you are always free to make your own. For the time being, let's take a look at some of the most common tarot spreads that are quick and easy to learn and perfect for beginners.

Three-Card Spreads

Three-card spreads are the easiest to learn and perform. You assign three spots in a line one after the other. The first card is laid down slightly to the reader's left. To the right of that, the second card is laid down. The third card is laid down to the right of the second. With that, you have the template for a three-card spread. You can take this to pretty much limitless possibilities. We'll cover five different three-card spreads that you can start using in minutes.

One great three-card spread that can help us to get a better sense of ourselves is the end / start / keep it up spread. The first card pulled tells us what we need to end. That could be an action that is holding us back, or a way in which our actions and attitudes have been hurting another. The second card is what we need to start doing. That will help us to repair the damage from what we had to stop. The final card is the keep it up card. When we find out that we need to end something, we often get hurt by this, and we forget that we are also doing a lot of good. This third card tells us the good that we've been doing and need to maintain. This spread lets us get a better sense of how we should behave, and how we should treat each other and ourselves as we move through life.

If you have a problem, then one of the best spreads is the situation / problem / advice spread. There are many similar spreads that help readers to get a better sense of the problem they are facing, but this one is particularly useful because it doesn't only look at the problem, but also takes into account the situation. Problems arise from, and as parts of, situations and not just as entities unto themselves. This spread starts by laying a card down to get a better sense of the situation, and only then does it move onto figuring out the nature of the problem and the method that will provide the cure. This will leave you not only with a way to approach the problem, but a better understanding of how the problem came to be in the first place.

If you are looking to get more in tune with yourself, then try a mind / body / spirit layout. If you are feeling lost or unsure of where you stand in the world, then this spread is perfect. The first card represents your mind, the next your body, and the third your spirit. Depending on what cards are drawn, you may find a way to get back in touch with each of these elements, or you may find you have not been acting in accordance with your beliefs. You may also find out what forces are preventing you from feeling comfortable in your skin again. Readings of this sort often come up with surprising results because what we believe ourselves to be, and what we really are, are rarely the same. If you approach a mind / body / spirit spread while tangled up in your ego, then you are more likely to avoid the truth the cards show you. Try to approach your readings with an open mind and soul, receptive to the knowledge you discover. Remember that knowledge is impartial, and so it doesn't always correspond to our hopes or beliefs.

If you are like me, then you are into heavy planning and have a schedule set up well ahead of time. If you like to set goals and aim for them, then you can get some advice for tackling these from the tarot deck. Using a now / want / how spread can be a great way to include the tarot in your planning. The first card helps you to get a sense of where you are now. The want card indicates the path you must learn and walk if you are to get to your goal. The how card tells you how you can get to that place, what skills and strengths you have that (if followed) will allow you to achieve your goal.

Finally, a strength / weakness / advice spread is another great way to get a sense of who you are in the present moment and what you are best at. We are often told to follow our strengths and let these guide us, but sometimes we can lose sight of what they are. That's especially true if we can't see a way to direct our strength to the current situation. A great soccer player might not be able to see how his skills on the field will help him when it comes to investing, but there are many skills we don't realize we have. That soccer player had to learn how to train and push themselves, and this sets them up for learning skills like investing. If you aren't sure what strengths you bring to your current situation, draw your first card to find out. Your second card will show you your weakness. The third is the advice card, which here offers a way of making your weakness into a strength itself.

TAROT FOR BEGINNERS

Love Spreads

Love is one of the great mysteries of our existence. Why we love and how we develop it makes about as much sense to the average person as it does to neuroscientists. Love is such an ethereal and confusing experience that it should come as no surprise that easily 50% of the questions tarot readers get are related to love in some way. Love or careers, they're the two biggies. We'll look at careers in a moment, but right now is the time for matters of the heart. We'll look at a couple of wonderful love spreads that you can use, starting with a three-card spread that builds off our previous conversation. Don't worry; we'll be getting up to seven-card spreads with this category, so we're going to give our skills a new challenge.

The easiest way to do a reading on love is to start with three cards and go from there. Do a me / them / dynamic spread. The first card represents who you are. What do you bring to the relationship? Is this what you actually bring, or have you gotten lost in misconceptions of your role? The second card represents your lover. It tells you what role they play while reminding you to consider if this is based in reality or your perceptions, and it asks you to consider how this spirals out to have an influence on your relationship. To get a better understanding of that relationship, we draw the third card. This card represents the dynamic of the relationship and helps you to get a sense of where its core is based. Knowing this allows you to stoke that core to keep the fires of love burning bright.

A more complicated spread is the five-card love spread. Here you have me / them / past / present / future. That is is a great card for getting a sense of where your relationship has been and where it is going. However, the cards are laid out in a slightly odd fashion. The first card is laid to the left like you were starting a three-card spread. The second card jumps the middle card that hasn't been laid yet so that the second card you play would be the final slot of a three-card spread. The third card is placed above the empty middle. The fourth card fills in the middle, and the fifth is laid to the bottom.

TAROT FOR BEGINNERS

This gives a very basic cross shape that can be used for many different spreads. But we're looking at a love spread, so let's get a sense of this.

The first card, laid to the far left, is the me card. That represents what you bring to the relationship and how you act. The second card, on the far right, represents your partner and what they bring to the relationship. The third card, the topmost position of the spread, represents the past which you have come from. The past is where the roots of the relationship are planted. Those roots are strong and grew up together for a reason; this card helps us to get back to that initial attraction and connection. The fourth card, in the middle, is the present. It is *now*, as of the reading, and it will tell you if the relationship is doing well or not. The bottom card is the fifth, and it is the immediate future for the relationship. Each of the four directions has an influence on the middle card, and so you can understand the middle card, the now you are living in, by realizing how each of the four pieces that influence it interact.

Our most complicated spread yet is called a compatibility spread. This spread helps you see how you and your partner interact and connect. There are pieces of interpersonal connection that we often miss in our conscious experience. Turning to the tarot deck can make this much easier. This spread isn't easy, however, as it uses seven cards to represent your wants / their wants / how you differ / how you are alike / if you are emotionally compatible / if you are physically compatible / if you are mentally compatible. To do this, the spread puts the first card down in the left position. Jump the middle and put the second card down to the far right of the first card. The third card is placed underneath the first card, and the fourth card is placed underneath the second. The fifth card is placed between the first and the second card. Place the fifth card so that it rests higher on the table than the first or the second, with the bottom half of the fifth card ending another in the middle of the first and second. Put the sixth card under the fifth, so that it's top half is halfway up the first and the second cards, and its bottom half is halfway down the third and fourth cards. Put the seventh and final card below the sixth so that its top half is halfway up the third and fourth cards. That will give you three columns lined up with two - three - two cards in them.

The first card you lay down represents what you want in a relationship, while the second card that is across from it is what your partner wants. The third card is your differences, and it helps you to understand where you are the most dissimilar. Perhaps that is a deal-breaker in the relationship or merely something to overcome. The fourth card is your similarities. This can help you see where you will bond and agree, but it can also show you that you have similarities that are negative as well. The connection cards make up five, six, and seven, and they let you know if you will be able to connect with each other on the level of your emotions, physicality, and mental prowess.

Career Spreads

Career spreads are among the most difficult of those you will encounter. There are other spreads that are more difficult, but the career spreads have many different unique spreads that will push a beginner's abilities. Considering many variables are involved in our careers, this shouldn't come as any surprise. It is precisely these variables that made us want to consult the tarot deck about our jobs in the first place, after all. We'll look at three spreads ranging from a pyramid to an ill-defined T, and one we use when we face problems in the workplace.

The pyramid spread can be helpful for several kinds of career-based questions. If you are trying to figure out where you should be aiming for the future, then this works, but it also works if you are trying to get a reminder of why you started doing this in the first place. Anytime that you need to get in touch with that profound sense of purpose and planning, a pyramid spread can help. This particular spread works by placing the first three cards in a line like a typical three-card spread. Card four and five are placed above it so that the middle of the card is lined up over the spaces between the first and the second cards and the second and third cards. The sixth and final card is placed at the very top with its middle placed in the space between the fourth and the fifth cards. This spread has the look of a game set up with playing cards rather than tarot cards.

The first card that you lay corresponds to your purpose, your reason for being in this field in the first place. The second card helps you to build on this by connecting you to the source of your motivations. The third card reminds you of your responsibilities and what role you are expected to have. Moving to the next row up, the fourth card is a project check-in. This card is the present; it is for you to get a sense of the environment you are in, and if you still enjoy it or not, if it still excites you in any way. The fifth card is the reward card, and it connects you to what rewards await you if you continue working in this particular career. The sixth and final card is the future, and it tells you where you are headed if you stay on this path. Are you after a career in this field and looking for a promotion, or are you trapped in a field you don't want to be in? Regardless of which is correct, you can find out where you are headed if you stick to this path. This spread might show you that you're going in the right direction, or it might demonstrate that you need a change; either way, you are better equipped with this new-found knowledge.

The next spread looks like an upside-down T, and it is used to get a sense of how we can find achievement. When we know where we want to go, this spread helps us to find a way there. It uses five cards with the first laid in the middle position. The second card is placed beneath the first, and the third is placed beneath the second. The fourth card is placed to the left of the third, while the fifth is placed to the right. That creates two lines of three cards each. These cards begin by helping you get a better sense of your dream job and then work on actualizing it.

The first card is correlated to your dream job. What you pull won't be your dream job itself, but it will give you a sense of how it will make you feel fulfilled and whether or not it is more in tune with the spiritual, the emotional, or the mental. The second card is the road that will lead you there; it tells you what parts of yourself you need to look to for the directions to your goal. The third card helps you to get a sense of how you fit into your dream job. What unique skills and abilities do you bring to the table? Draw and place the third card to find out. The fourth card points you towards the helpers. These might be friends, family, coworkers, strangers, or even parts of yourself. Wherever help rests, the fourth card will point towards it. The fifth and final card is the attention card; it tells you what you have forgotten and what will soon be a problem. When read, you get a solid understanding of how to achieve your career goals.

Our final spread is designed to help solve the problems that crop up again and again in the workplace. It is also the first spread that we've used, which involves laying or stacking cards onto each other. The first card is laid in the middle, and the second card is laid on its side overtop of the first so that it creates the shape of a cross. The third card is placed to the left of this, the fourth card is placed to the right. The fifth card is placed above the first and second, and the sixth card is placed below them. This creates a cross shape which has a smaller cross in its middle. There are many spreads that stack cards above each other, so this shouldn't be considered a radical placement by any stretch of the imagination.

TAROT FOR BEGINNERS

The first card placed represents your goal, the answer you are looking for. In this spread, this is most often the solution to the problem you are trying to deal with. The second card, the one laid over the first, is the challenge that is preventing you from acting. Keep in mind that this card is naturally laying down, and so this can change the way you interpret it. The third card represents what is holding you back and stopping you from being your most efficient. The fourth card is the opposite, and it represents what is pulling you forward and helping you to keep going and being the most productive you can be. The fifth card looks at what you get out of your job. That ranges from the money to the satisfaction to the frustration and disappointment, all and everything that the job provides. The sixth and final card represents the factors that are affecting the entire spread, those elements you can't see directly, but which are impacting and making the problem worse. When you take these all together, you can solve any career-centered problem you face with the wisdom of the tarot.

Chapter Summary

- Spreads are simply ways of arranging the cards in order to get an answer from them.

- Each location in the spread has its meaning, which alters the way the card is to be read.

- The easiest spreads to do are three-card spreads. One card to the left, one in the middle, and one to the right.

- Three-card spreads can be used for just about any topic you can think of, but they won't be able to give you elaborate detail on the topic.

- Common topics for spreads include love and careers.

- There are many spreads with five or more cards, which all interact with each other to produce their complete meaning.

- Practice more difficult spreads first on your own before working them on other people.

- Cards are often laid over the top of each other to create alternative meanings to each other.

In the next chapter, you will learn all the terminology that you've encountered throughout the book and that you'll face once you start talking about tarot cards out there in the real world.

CHAPTER SIX

GLOSSARY

There are a lot of words and terms when it comes to tarot card reading, so, hopefully, this glossary will come in handy. It's packed full of all the weird words you'll find in this book, as well as many that are floating around out there, which we didn't even have time to get into just yet. It's my hope that you'll find this chapter paying off, even after you are well beyond the status of beginner.

Air: The unseeable element, considered to be magical and represented in the minor arcana by the wand suit.

Akasha: Also known as spirit, another intangible element that is considered to be magical, though not directly assigned to a suit.

TAROT FOR BEGINNERS

Altar: Any surface that is set aside for use with only a certain ritual. A priest stands in front of an altar when they give Mass, though this altar is representative of power to those in the Christian faith. An altar can have magical power, though often its power is the personal or spiritual significance the altar has. Some tarot users only read the cards on their altar.

Aquarius: One of the Zodiac signs, for people born between January 21 and February. Said to have a connection to air.

Aries: One of the Zodiac signs, for people born between March 21 and April 20. Said to have a connection to fire.

Baton: The minor arcana suit that we have been referring to as wands.

Cancer: One of the Zodiac signs, for people born between June 22 and July 22. Said to have a connection to water.

Capricorn: One of the Zodiac signs, for people born between December 23 and January 20. Said to have a connection to earth.

Cartomancy: This is the name given to the art of using cards to read the future. This can be done with any type of card, including tarot cards, but it is not directly related to the art of reading tarot card spreads.

Chalice: The minor arcana suit that we have been referring to as cups.

Clubs: The minor arcana suit that we have been referring to as wands. Clubs is the French name, which made its way into modern-day playing cards.

Coins: A suit of the minor arcana. It is known as diamonds in the French, has a connection to earth and merchants, as well as the physical body or your possessions.

Consultant: A tarot card reader is sometimes called a consultant because they "consult the cards" for advice and solutions to your problems.

Court Cards: The page, knight, queen, and king from each minor arcana suit. These correspond loosely to the face cards in a deck of playing cards. They may have different names, and so "court cards" is a catch-all to refer to their position rather than their individual title in a deck.

Cups: A suit of the minor arcana. It is also known as hearts in the French, has a connection to water and the clergy, as well as emotions and love.

Devil's Picture Book: This was a derogatory name given to tarot cards, though in recent years, it has been taken as an ironic badge of honor by many.

Dignified: A term used to describe a card that is placed down in a standing position.

Disks: The minor arcana suit that we have been referring to as cups.

Divination: The art of telling the future through the use of some kind of tool. While cartomancy specifically uses cards, divination can be carried out through casting stones or many other ways. For example, cartomancy is a subtype of divination.

Earth: The ground, trees, and nature. Earth is associated with the suit of coins and is considered one of the elements to hold its own source of magic.

Fire: The flame and the sun. Fire is associated with the suit of wands, and is considered one of the elements to hold its own source of magic.

Fool's Journey: The tarot deck begins with the fool. The fool's journey is a story of the fool traveling through the other 21 cards of the major arcana. It is a fun story to learn, and telling it with the cards can make for a captivating party trick.

Golden Dawn: A group of occultists that studied magic in the Western world. A.E. Waite and P. Coleman Smith met as members and formed two-thirds of the group behind the Rider-Waite tarot deck, as Waite provided the knowledge, and Smith illustrated the cards.

Hearts: The minor arcana suit that we have been referring to as Cups. Hearts is the French name, which made its way into modern playing cards.

Ill Dignified: One way of referring to a card that is played with the front of the card down.

Intuitive Reading: Most of the time, we ask the tarot cards a question and then translate the answer through the cards. An intuitive reading is when you spread the cards without a question in mind and see what they are saying on their own.

Leo: One of the Zodiac signs, for people born between July 23 and August 21. Said to have a connection to fire.

Libra: One of the Zodiac signs, for people born between September 24 and October 23. Said to have a connection to air.

Little White Book: The little white book is a shorthand way of referring to the instructional manual that comes with a set of playing cards. While many decks no longer have a white manual, the most popular ones did, and the nickname stuck.

Major Arcana: The 22 trump cards in the deck that begin with the fool and represent the fool's journey through life and awareness.

Minor Arcana: 56 cards split into four suits of 14 cards, each ranging from ace to king. They are like a normal set of playing cards except that they go 10, page, knight, queen, and king at the end. Each of the 56 cards has its meaning, but, most often, they modify elements of the major arcana.

Numerology: Numerology is a form of divination that sees portents in numbers and believes these have great value in seeing the future. Numerologists may use the tarot deck in their readings, but this is not a normal function of the tarot deck itself.

Oracle Deck: An oracle deck is similar to a tarot deck, but it is more interested in reading peoples' fortunes. Each deck is unique, and they haven't been around nearly as long as tarot cards have either.

Path: Path sometimes refers to the magical path that one walks in one's life, but it can also represent the 22 possibilities of the major arcana.

Pentacles: The minor arcana suit that we have been referring to as coins.

Pip: All the cards of the minor arcana are numbered. Some sets include these numbers, and others require you to memorize the card's meaning. The pip refers to the number of the card itself, and, secondly, the part of the card that it is written on.

Pisces: One of the Zodiac signs, for people born between February 20 and March 20. Said to have a connection to water.

Querent: Divination may be practiced alone, but it is most often practiced with a client or friend that has things they need to know about the future. When this is the case, the person with the questions is the querent.

Reader: The reader is the person who draws the cards, lays the spread, and reads the results.

Reversed Card: A card that is reversed may be upside down or backward, the same as an ill dignified card.

Rods: The minor arcana suit that we have been referring to as wands.

Runes: Dating back much further than the tarot, runes were symbols carved into small but hard surfaces that could be rolled like dice or spread out like cards to perform acts of divination.

Sagittarius: One of the Zodiac signs, for people born between November 23 and December 22. Said to have a connection to fire.

Scepters: The minor arcana suit that we have been referring to as wands.

TAROT FOR BEGINNERS

Significator: When an act of divination is happening through the cards, often, the person asking the question will be given a card that represents them through the rest of the reading. This card becomes the central element, and the others then modify and interact with it.

Spades: The minor arcana suit that we have been referring to as swords. Spades is the French name, which made its way into modern-day playing cards

Spirit: One of the magical elements, along with fire, earth, water, and air.

Spread: The way in which the tarot cards are laid down. Each location of a spread has a particular meaning that affects the meaning of the cards laid down there.

Staves: The minor arcana suit that we have been referring to as wands.

Swords: A suit of the minor arcana. It is also known as spades in the French, has a connection to water and the nobility and the military, as well as reason.

Tarot Cards: The 22 trump cards referred to as the major arcana and 56 cards of the minor arcana, which are split into four suits of 14 cards each. The cards each have a particular meaning and help us to get in touch with our inner wisdom.

Tarot Deck: The tarot deck is the 78 cards made up of the major and minor arcana.

Taurus: One of the Zodiac signs, for people born between April 21 and May 21. Said to have a connection to earth.

Virgo: One of the Zodiac signs, for people born between August 22 and September 23. Said to have a connection to earth.

Wands: A suit of the minor arcana. It is also known as clubs in the French, has a connection to fire and builders, as well as creativity and willpower.

Water: One of the magical elements, along with fire, earth, air, and spirit.

FINAL WORDS

While the tarot deck is surrounded by mystique and mythology, it isn't any more complicated than most card games. But the tarot deck isn't a game, so much as it is a tool for understanding yourself and the wisdom you hold. The tarot deck will point you towards the answers inside of yourself and show you the truths that you didn't want to face. These cards offer advice and wisdom that can let us live a much fuller and more fulfilling life.

The first step to using the tarot deck is to stop giving power to the myths surrounding it. We look at the history of the tarot deck and these myths themselves in the first chapter so that we can cut away all the misunderstandings and get to the core truth at hand. This then set us up so that we could pick our own deck, learn how to ask questions of the deck, and get a sense of how spread and position affect meaning in chapter two.

With a solid understanding of the deck in hand, we turned our attention towards the cards themselves to get a sense of how decks differ from each other, and how the major and minor arcanas function. Since this made up chapter three, chapter four was free to explore the meanings of each and every one of the 78 cards we use as a part of the tarot deck. We can't read the cards until we know the cards, and this chapter is one that you'll want to study until you are comfortable and have integrated the knowledge into a part of yourself.

We closed out on chapter five, where we learned how to do some of the more common spreads in tarot. These ranged from simple three-card spreads to complicated spreads of five or more cards with overlapping cards, and specific rules surrounding placement. Just because these already have rules on how to use them, you shouldn't think anything is holding you back from making your own. Follow what you feel, always.

The thing with the tarot deck is that rules and guidelines are never as important as what you feel and understand to be true in your heart. Your relationship to your cards might look nothing like another reader's, and that is perfectly fine. So long as you respect the cards and understand them, you are free to use them in whatever way they call out to you. I hope that you have learned enough to get started performing your own readings and that I am lucky enough to receive one myself someday.

www.ingramcontent.com/pod-product-compliance
Lightning Source LLC
Chambersburg PA
CBHW052057110526
44591CB00013B/2243